THE ELEANOR CROSSES

THE ELEANOR CROSSES

The Story of King Edward I's Lost Queen and her Architectural Legacy

Decca Warrington

Signal Books
Oxford

First published in 2018 by
Signal Books Limited
36 Minster Road
Oxford OX4 1LY
www.signalbooks.co.uk

A catalogue record for this book is available from the British Library

ISBN 978-1-909930-65-0 Paper

Cover Design: Tora Kelly
Production: Tora Kelly
Cover Image: James Basire, *The cross erected in memory of Queen Eleanor, near Waltham* (1903), Library of Congress, Washington DC
Map: Sebastian Ballard
Printed in India by Imprint Digital

CONTENTS

This book is for Haydn, with love and thanks.

INTRODUCTION

On 27 November 1290 the Queen of England, Eleanor of Castile, died unexpectedly in the tiny, previously unremarkable Nottinghamshire village of Harby. Her devastated husband, King Edward I, whom she had been accompanying on his travels northwards to the neighbouring kingdom of Scotland, found himself turning around and taking a very different journey: the grim procession of Eleanor's funeral cortège to her final resting place in London's Westminster Abbey.

The first section of this book follows the course of that journey, a gruelling undertaking in the depths of winter, with harsh realities that are difficult for us to comprehend. But the barriers to our understanding relate to more than just practicalities. In that medieval world, where attitudes and ideas were so different from those of the twenty-first century, much of the prevailing mind-set seems strange. Of the universally held beliefs of the time, some seem laughable, some repellent even. Yet if we can be allowed to make a leap of imagination and step back through the centuries we may discover human impulses that are familiar: love, grief, fear, superstition, creativity and passion. To these and more we can undoubtedly respond.

For the people who were part of the cortège - royalty, nobility and servants alike — this was a journey of momentous importance. The route of that journey had no intrinsic significance before 1290. But Eleanor's grief-stricken husband was to mark it out, he hoped forever, with a building project of unparalleled scale and imagination. King Edward's vision was to construct an elaborate stone memorial cross at the journey's start and at each of its overnight stopping places, twelve in total: love letters cast in stone to his devoted wife of thirty-six years. Each one over fifty feet tall, these crosses were intended not only to be visible reminders of the queen's departed soul, but focal points for the prayers of all who saw them.

THE ELEANOR CROSSES

The end of that medieval journey was, however, only the beginning of another story: that of the crosses themselves.

The second section of this book takes up their narrative through more than seven hundred years of history. Each of the twelve crosses that Edward built has its own story—stories that collectively tell much about major changes at key periods in English history. But they also provide a narrative of survival and continuity, representing keyholes that allow us glimpses back to the past, giving tantalising insights into the history of the nation. Nine crosses have been lost to us, but even their absence leaves echoes.

But what, finally, can we retrieve about the life of Eleanor herself, the woman who inspired so monumental a legacy? The third section of this book pieces together the story of her marriage to Edward, a marriage of exceptional devotion. When left a widower, King Edward went to unprecedented lengths to immortalise Eleanor. It is that marriage, the catalyst for the creation of the Eleanor Crosses, which is at the heart of the whole story.

Part 1

THE DEATH OF A QUEEN

1.

A JOURNEY DIVERTED

The King and Queen of England, accompanied by their entourage, have set out northwards from Clipstone in Nottinghamshire where the Parliament of October 1290 has recently concluded. King Edward I is riding towards the front, his wife and cherished companion, Queen Eleanor of Castile, by his side. As always, it is with her that King Edward wishes to discuss the debates held, agreements forged and his ambitions for the future. And for this giant of a king, over six foot two inches tall, there are ambitions in plenty. Although fifty-one years old, King Edward has the energy of a man half his age and shows no signs of being ready to rest.

The royal couple are in celebratory mood, jubilant that the negotiations with the magnates, always delicate and sometimes confrontational, have been concluded to the king's satisfaction. Talking over the decisions taken, they are united in their delight that the lords of the realm have agreed to raise the large sums of money needed for a crusade to the Holy Land. King Edward is to receive £130,000 that has already been collected and he will also be given the proceeds of a new six-year tax. The date for departure has been set for summer 1293, allowing less than three years for preparation.

For Edward this new endeavour is an opportunity to complete the unfinished business of the crusade that he and Eleanor were part of twenty years before. That attempt to save the holy cities, with the alluring prize of Jerusalem, was thwarted by insufficient military strength to confront the enemy. Since that time Edward has never wavered in his ambition to be remembered as a great Christian warrior king, rescuer of the Holy Land from occupation by the Mamluk Muslim infidel. Eleanor has always given him every encouragement, imagining him surpassing the great conquests of her father, Ferdinand III of Castile. She is determined to accompany him again, undeterred by having now reached her fiftieth year. Edward, as he has so often been, is proud of his spirited wife and glad that she will be there to support and advise him.

The royal party is now heading towards Haddington in the Scottish lowlands, 250 miles and perhaps two weeks of arduous travel away. As a highly respected monarch with experience of diplomacy across realms, King Edward has been invited to meet the lords of the independent Kingdom of Scotland. He is to give his advice on a critical moment for the royal succession in the aftermath of the death of King Alexander III.

The crisis was sparked earlier that autumn, when Alexander's granddaughter and heir — a seven-year-old Norwegian princess - fell ill and died while sailing to Scotland for her coronation. The devastating death of Margaret the Maid of Norway now makes it necessary to delve back over a hundred years into King Alexander's ancestry to find an alternative successor. A number of conflicting claims to the throne have emerged and Edward's advice has been sought to assess their validity. He also has a personal interest, as his own six-year-old son and heir, Prince Edward of Caernarvon, and the deceased Maid Margaret, were betrothed to be married - a union that was intended to bring the two neighbouring kingdoms together in natural alliance.

Travel during these winter months is always unpredictable, likely to be frustratingly delayed by inclement weather with flooding making some routes impassable. But on this occasion the progress is slowed still further as Eleanor succumbs to bouts of feverish illness. Although inconvenienced, the king and queen are not at first unduly perturbed as she has suffered similarly before yet made a full recovery. Eleanor is anxious that her ill-health will not slow the entourage down, but as they press on northwards the periods of sicknesses become more frequent and intense, with alarming bouts of hot fever. Such is her discomfort that it is soon difficult for the queen to travel at all, since her aching limbs leave her unable to support herself on horseback.

The royal physician, Henry de Montepessulano, is summoned urgently to attend the queen. King Edward has great faith in the effectiveness of his remedies. He was so impressed by his superior knowledge that the king brought him many years ago from the royal lands in Gascony to join the English court. Even though no expense is spared for his recommended syrups and medicines, on this occasion his treatments are of no avail. To the deepening alarm of the king and queen, the times of release from fever are no more than occasional moments of respite.

As fears grow the king decides to abandon his plans and heads east instead of north, with the destination of Lincoln Cathedral in mind. Once there, the royal couple plan to seek the intervention of St Hugh, former Bishop of Lincoln and patron saint of the sick, shoemakers and swans. He was regarded as the wisest bishop in the country at the time of his death in 1200, ninety years before. They are pinning their hopes upon praying for salvation at his shrine, trusting that St Hugh will look favourably on their plea and intercede with God on their behalf. Both Edward and Eleanor were present on the occasion of the translation of the saint's remains to a splendid new tomb ten years previously. They desperately hope that the honours St Hugh was then shown will encourage him to help them now, when Eleanor's need of divine intervention is becoming ever more desperate.

As the ribbon of travellers threads its way through the seemingly endless flat country of Lincolnshire, Eleanor is at times too unwell even to be carried on a litter, the uneven ground making the horses stumble, jolting her fragile body. The entourage shudders to a halt, the will of the king unable to drive it forwards.

*

THE ELEANOR CROSSES

On 20 November, several weeks after leaving Clipstone, the city of Lincoln, with the promise of salvation it surely offers, is tantalisingly close, a mere ten miles away. But it is clear that their objective is at least for now unreachable and as the main entourage creaks painfully forwards, the royal messenger rides ahead to the nearby village of Harby. He is to warn the owner of the manor that the King of England will soon be at his door and in need of hospitality.

The settlement is similar to thousands of others, perhaps half a dozen meagre wood-framed cottages clustered together in the forest clearing. Set slightly apart is the sombre, grey stone church and manor house, the buildings wrapped in an all-embracing dankness, the smell of wood smoke sitting low.

The manor house, the only dwelling of more than two rooms, is the home of a knight, Richard de Weston. Although rich to the ordinary villagers, Richard is far from being among the wealthy and powerful of the land and is not accustomed to receiving grand visitors. Yet it is here that the royal party must stop, clinging to the hope that a few days of rest and medication will allow Eleanor to resume the journey to Lincoln.

Richard is roused from sleep by shouts and a pounding on the door. Baffled by the commotion, he hears his servant open the door, the chill wind of the November night whistling through the house. He drags a cover around himself and goes to find what the shouting is about. Richard is astonished to find a man looming out of the darkness at the top of the steps leading to the entrance, who announces himself as the messenger of the king. He is ordered to prepare himself for the arrival of the royal party, now a mere hour away. At first he cannot believe it is true, but the messenger shows him the king's seal, shouting at him to busy himself. Shocked by the urgency of the instructions, Richard must accept that the King and Queen of England truly are on their way to his home, most certainly an honour he never sought nor wished for.

He, in turn, shouts to his wife to vacate their bedchamber, aware of the paltriness of his home in comparison to the palaces and great houses to which the guests are accustomed. With only a few rooms in the manor, he instructs the servant to prepare a makeshift bed in one of the out buildings for himself and his wife, giving up his bedchamber for the king and queen, the hall for the distinguished members of the royal retinue. They rekindle the fire in the hall and light bonfires around the house in readiness for the impending arrival. With inadequate shelter under their roof, many of their servants will have to huddle around the fires to sleep as best they can while the royal attendants occupy the ground floor cellar below the kitchen.

Before Richard has time fully to understand what is happening, more travellers start pouring into his home. He is waiting at the door as the towering figure of a man comes towards him. Struck speechless, he is roughly pushed forward by one of the attendants, telling him to greet his monarch. He bows deeply, the words refusing to leave his mouth. Richard is uncertain that his legs will hold him, fear reducing them to melting candle wax. The King of England himself enters his house, stooping to get his vast frame through its door. The tiny form of a woman is then carried in. This, he understands, is his sick queen and his house has become her shelter for as long as need be.

*

As the cycle of long days passes into the next week, Lincoln and the hope it offered just a short while before become a distant dream. For most of the party, these dark dreary days seem endless, but for Edward time loses all meaning. His love for Eleanor has been essential to him all his adult life. Since he was fifteen and she thirteen they have given each other strength and hope, rarely separated except through war and imprisonment, sharing the triumphs and tragedies.

THE ELEANOR CROSSES

He cannot bear to leave her bedside, watching helplessly as her condition worsens, her body dripping with hot sweats. In spite of his habitual restlessness and impatience, he remains devotedly beside her, desperate to offer what comfort he can.

It is evident to all that the queen's condition is grave, as she certainly would not consider staying in Harby if there were any possibility of travelling onwards to reach somewhere with greater comforts. During the long days and nights as the fever takes hold of her there are times when Eleanor believes herself to be transported to her native Castile, the country she left after her marriage when she was thirteen years old. She mutters incoherently about her home in Burgos, imagining the summer heat weighing heavy on her skin, the sweet smell of orange groves in her nostrils. More alarming still are the times when she confuses the heat she is feeling with the fires of Purgatory. Even though she is weakened by illness her distress is so great that she finds the strength to cry out in fear.

There are some moments of lucidity but they do not bring Eleanor peace. Rather, to Edward's distress, she expresses great agitation, speaking of her growing conviction that there is to be no cure. For Eleanor is truly frightened, certain that she faces death and terrified by what the after-life will bring. Although she does not sincerely believe she has done such wrong that she will be condemned to eternal damnation in Hell, her apprehension about how her sins will be judged will not allow her rest.

She speaks in trepidation of Purgatory, the place between Heaven and Hell where all souls go after death. For those who have committed mortal sin there is no hope. They, the damned, are destined to be sent from Purgatory directly to Hell, the place from which there is no return, no reprieve, no possibility of salvation. An eternity of anguish is their inevitable fate. The saints will also pass through Purgatory, but for them the stay will only be brief. They will not be touched by its tortures, as they make their way to eternal peace in Heaven. All the rest, those who are neither unforgivably wicked nor saintly, will remain in Purgatory. There they will stay whilst their souls are painfully cleansed of the sins of their time on earth for which atonement can be made, before they are allowed to pass through into Heaven.

In its time in Purgatory the soul will be painfully stripped of its wrongdoing, purged by fire, ice or knives, the method according to the sin, the suffering made worse by noxious smells and ghastly shrieks piercing the blackness. Although no one can know in advance exactly how long the suffering will be or what form it will take, it is certain that it will be agonising. For Eleanor and Edward, royal blood offers no escape from this process, all sinners being equal in the eyes of God. For them, as for their humblest servants, the greater the sins committed during life on earth, the longer the soul will have to suffer in Purgatory.

One small way in which the torments that lie ahead can be reduced is by enduring heat while waiting for death to strike. In that knowledge the queen is kept covered in heavy blankets with the fire constantly smouldering, even though she is burning up with fever. In spite of the November chill outside, in that room everyone feels the heat of the fire, its crackling mocking their discomfort, the smoke stinging their eyes. Still Edward will not move from the bedside of his adored Eleanor, this normally restless man rendered immobile.

As the queen's agitation grows she clutches Edward's arm, begging for help. Edward tries as best he can to soothe her, to give her consolation. He speaks calmly of his conviction that she is not to blame for the sins she supposes she will be held to account for. But Eleanor, with the certainty that she is facing death, finds herself unable to look into her heart without regretting some of her actions. She will, she knows, die a wealthy woman and is fearful that her property is tarnished with dishonour. For as queen, she, with Edward's full knowledge and encouragement, built up significant property holdings through the acquisition of the debts of impecunious land owners. Now that images of Purgatory are looming, she is fearful that there have been times when she, and bailiffs acting on her behalf, were too harsh on those unfortunate people who found themselves in financial hardship. Perhaps she was too intolerant of late payments, too unquestioning of her bailiffs' methods of extracting her dues.

Desperate to offer comfort, Edward searches for words of reassurance, reminding her that the motivation for her actions was in essence honourable. They have many times discussed her future should Edward predecease her. As queen consort she receives only a paltry income, allowed to her by Parliament, in her own right. Were she to have been a dowager queen she would have lost even this small allowance and would have been dependent for income on the properties held in her own name. So Eleanor, with Edward's support and agreement, took steps to ensure that she would be financially secure in this eventuality.

Now released from the perils of childbearing, this was the future that Edward and Eleanor imagined to be most likely. It was Edward who was the elder by two years and, as king, more at risk from violent attack. Yet even though Edward's life has indeed been threatened on a number of occasions, his luck has been remarkable and it now seems that it is she who will be taken first.

If left a widow, Eleanor would also have taken on the significant responsibility of providing guidance to their infant son, Edward of Caernarvon, on succeeding to his father's throne. Such a role was taken by many previous dowager queens and was one for which Eleanor's intelligence and experience would have equipped her well.

While therefore considering her land acquisitions justifiable, Eleanor cannot have been unaware of criticisms levelled against her. Indeed, the Archbishop of Canterbury, John Pecham, once wrote to her, raising concerns that her actions could be perceived as being motivated by self-interested greed. He even suggested that she could be considered guilty of usury, a practice explicitly condemned in the Bible.

The unpredictable nature of her illness having denied her the opportunity to acquit herself of sin in her own lifetime, Eleanor finds herself approaching death with desperate anxiety. She has heard that the punishment for usury is to be boiled in molten gold and is terrified that her actions should be judged as warranting such treatment. Who could tell what other sins she might be held accountable for? Perhaps she will be found guilty of pride for which the punishment is to be bound to revolving iron wheels, covered with burning hooks.

In an effort to find her some spiritual comfort, a servant is dispatched to fetch the priest, William de Kelm, from the Church of All Saints that stands opposite the manor. He reads to her from the prayer book that she keeps with her on her travels. Eleanor finds some relief in the familiar words. The young priest reassures her that a future in Heaven does eventually await her. Although no one can tell for how long Purgatory will have to be endured, its pains imply salvation, for those who undergo its punishments will eventually be cleansed. The presence of this man of God, though inexperienced, gives Eleanor some slight reassurance.

During those dark hours, with the little breath she has left in her body, Eleanor prays to the saints to absolve her from sin, using such precious time as might be left to ask for their assistance in guarding the onward passage of her soul. She prays most fervently to those saints she has made offerings to, generously so, in her lifetime. Surely now they will return her patronage.

Eleanor is comforted to know that the power of the prayers of the living can be set against the sins of those poor suffering souls in Purgatory and reduce their time in that terrible place. With this knowledge she begs Edward to help her, entreating him to continue the prayers for her soul once she has departed, to help her through the inevitable terrors of that place.

For Edward, this is not the time to dwell on his own feelings of despair at watching the woman he has loved for so long slip away from him. He does all he can to offer comfort, assuring her that he will use his considerable power to make sure that she will always be remembered in prayer. Edward also promises that he will honour her memory by providing a tomb to match that of any Queen of England, a tomb of such splendour that it will draw many of the faithful to pray for her. Her body will, he tells her, be buried in Westminster Abbey, the place where he was christened and where they were jointly crowned. He describes a great monument for her. It will stand proudly alongside the shrine of his namesake, the sainted King Edward the Confessor, uncle of William the Conqueror and link to the noble history of the Anglo-Saxon rulers of England whose dynasty ended over two hundred years previously. She will, in death, receive the deserved devotion and prayers from her people that may not have been offered to her during her lifetime. Even Edward, with all his power to summon the best physicians in his lands, cannot save her life, but he can ensure prayers for her soul for all time.

Feeling the pain of her fear almost as if it were his own, he is passionate in his undertaking that he will rectify any wrongs done not only by her but in her name. Edward gives his fervent promise that he will be unswerving in his undertaking that everyone, whatever their rank, will be given an opportunity to put their case for grievance for harsh treatment at the hands of her bailiffs. He assures her that anyone with genuine claims will be fully compensated, however long ago the case occurred. His words are of some help to Eleanor, who knows so well that she can trust the strength of his love for her and knows, after so many years together, that he will do his utmost to honour his word.

On the night of 27 November the end is evidently near. A messenger is sent on horseback, travelling through the darkness to fetch the Bishop of Lincoln, Oliver Sutton. Edward and William de Kelm remain at Eleanor's bedside throughout the night, their insistent prayers repeated continuously, desperate for them to be heard.

The bishop has long been known to the king and queen, having presided at the consecration of the cathedral's new tomb of St Hugh. His position in the Church gives him suitable authority to perform the final sacrament of extreme unction, the ritual of anointing with holy oil to heal the soul before its departure.

The bishop arrives a few hours later, thankfully in time to administer the last rites. The king is grateful at least to have the opportunity to be with Eleanor at the very end, to allay her fears, to reassure her that they will in time be together in Heaven.

But in spite of all his words, the end is no gentle slipping away. Eleanor leaves the world with an abrupt shudder, eyes open, gasping with fear, a look of horror on her face at the very moment of her death that surely tells of a glimpse into Purgatory.

*

With Eleanor torn away from him so shockingly, Edward is left stunned, unspeakably bereaved. He has not yet begun to imagine his own future, a world without her. Haunted by the fear written across her face, he is certain that his capacity for joy has died with her. For how can he rest with images of the terrible suffering that Eleanor is at the same moment enduring? She has left for the next world, taking part of him with her and leaving him with the burden of responsibility for protecting her soul.

Until now, with his sixty-seven-year-old mother still alive, Edward has not begun to countenance the idea of the loss of his wife, a woman until recently so full of energy. They hoped she would also have many years ahead of her with the freedom to enjoy some of the privileges of royalty alongside him. He knows how much more he has received from her beyond the requirements of duty and obligation, how fortunate he has been to have her for his wife. Not only did she without complaint bear him sixteen children over thirty years, but she was also a constant source of advice and comfort. Together they shared profound grief at the death of eleven of those children, some as tiny infants, others as seemingly healthy children on whom they had pinned hopes for the future.

The Eleanor Crosses

Throughout their marriage of thirty-six years there was no official requirement for Edward to spend more time with Eleanor than the formalities of court etiquette demanded, yet theirs was no typical royal union. Of all the many companions he could choose from, it was she whom he preferred to spend his leisure time with, whether out hunting, reading or playing chess together. Together they travelled thousands of miles, through England, Wales and Scotland and across the seas to France, Genoa, Pisa, Sicily, Sardinia, Cyprus, North Africa and the Holy Land, content in each other's company. Now he finds himself left behind as she embarks upon her final journey.

As the long hours of night go on, Edward continues to sit with her lifeless corpse in quiet prayer. He is oblivious to his surroundings in this simple room, its wooden shutters inadequate to block the howling November wind, which became the antechamber to the after-life for the Queen of England. When the unkind light of morning comes, he stays beside her, refusing food, refusing to sleep. He is numbed by the cruelty of what has happened, not yet able to accept the reality. His advisers speak to him gently, trying to persuade him to allow Eleanor's body to be moved.

Time is precious even in death. The body must be embalmed before it can be taken on the long journey to London and its final resting place. He finds thinking about what must now be done almost unbearably painful. The king refuses to be hurried, needing this time for his own thoughts, struggling with the truth that Eleanor has gone.

It is a full four days of barely eating or sleeping before he can acknowledge the inevitable next steps and allow the corpse to be removed to St Katherine's Priory for its evisceration and embalmment. He will then accompany the body of the queen on their final journey together, distraught that the destination is not to be Scotland but Westminster Abbey and the occasion, her funeral.

The monks of St Katherine's Priory are sent a message that the queen has died and that they are to prepare themselves for receiving her mortal remains. They wait in anticipation. When no coffin arrives the next day or the day after that, they wonder if it can be true. At last, on the fourth day of rumours, word reaches them that a solemn procession is nearing. The pattern of their normally rigid daily routines is disrupted as they walk out to meet it, and the coffin is borne back to the priory, accompanied by the mournful ringing of bells and chanting of prayers.

The friar gives some of the older monks the task of carrying out the process of embalming. The responsibility with which they are entrusted is a heavy burden, requiring them to handle the corpse of the queen herself in such a brutal way. They respectfully lift the rigid body onto the trestle table of the priory kitchens, plunging into the naked flesh with their sharpest knives. They open up the body to reveal the internal organs and carefully remove the heart and viscera. These are respectfully placed in lidded wooden vessels. They then pad the cavity with herbs and barley.

The occasion is watched over by Bishop Sutton. Throughout the grim procedure he continues to offer prayers to safeguard the soul of the queen while her body is being reduced to its parts. One of the monks is charged with keeping the many censers burning, the pungent smoke carrying their prayers up to Heaven while disguising the nauseating smell. The monks have to cover their faces to stop themselves gagging.

When this task is finished the bones are returned over the body cavity and the skin pulled back over so that the corpse looks as undamaged as possible. It is then carefully dressed in fine linen robes and sprinkled with holy water before it is returned to its coffin. The queen is now prepared for the day of judgement, her earthly body complete.

The monks carry the precious remains in sombre procession up the steep hill towards the cathedral at its summit. Its three imposing towers break the skyline, a vision of the New Jerusalem, the spiritual community of Heaven as it appears on earth.

Such is the gradient of the ascent that six men have to hold the coffin to prevent it slipping. They pass flimsy wooden buildings that cling onto the slope as if one rainstorm might wash them down to the River Witham below. They reach the plateau at the top, the huge, louring stone castle on their left, opposite the gate into the cathedral yard. As they enter the yard the vast expanse of the west front of the cathedral itself stretches out before them. Its size and complexity never fails to astonish, so wide that their eyes have to scan from side to side to take in its full extent. Moving closer, the richness of the surface, decorated with sculptures illustrating the stories of the Old and New Testaments, statues of kings and saints, come into view. They enter the building by the central doorway, set within an arch fit for giants.

*

A service is held in the Angel Choir of Lincoln Cathedral, the sacred place that was Eleanor's destination during the final stages of her illness, such a different kind of service than Edward imagined. On his instructions, it is here that Eleanor's viscera are to be interred. For this magnificent part of the cathedral was built by the king's father, Henry III, to hold the shrine of St Hugh. Here the aura of reverence around the relics of the saint will protect the bodily remains of Eleanor. Throughout the night the monks watch over the coffin, chanting their prayers for the queen's soul, incense burning, candles flickering.

Plans are rapidly made for the arduous journey south, the timing of Eleanor's death during the months of severe weather making the 160-mile distance to Westminster Abbey seem daunting. The journey can be completed in a week if conditions are fair but it is important that the cortège stops at some of the principal abbeys of the land so that due respect can be shown to the departed queen. With this in mind, London is perhaps ten nights away.

Edward's advisers encourage him to stay and rest before embarking on the journey, leaving the Bishop of Lincoln, other men of the Church and trusted lords to accompany the body of Eleanor. But Edward is insistent on walking with the procession, believing that to do otherwise would not show her true honour on this unique and final journey. He will keep her coffin close by him as the cortège slowly makes its way south along the familiar roads. This time the royal party will be required to stop each night at a place where the coffin can rest safely in consecrated ground, secure within the body of a church where it will be protected by the Holy Spirit. Whatever is in store over the following days, it is certain that the journey ahead will be gruelling.

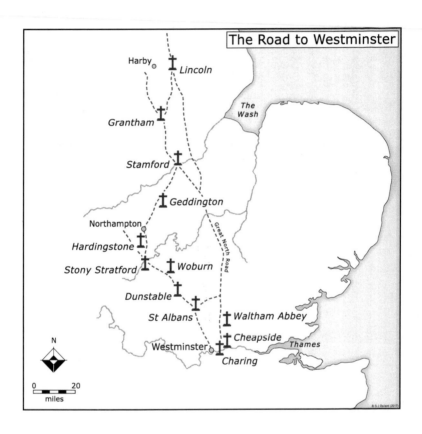

The Road to Westminster

Harby Lincoln

The Wash

Grantham

Stamford

Geddington

Northampton

Hardingstone

Great North Road

Stony Stratford Woburn

Dunstable

St Albans

Waltham Abbey

Cheapside

Westminster Thames

Charing

N

0   20
miles

2.

A MOURNFUL JOURNEY

It is still dark the next morning when the massive west doors of Lincoln Cathedral are heaved fully open for the funeral procession to spill out. The cortège weaves its way back down the hill and sets out towards Grantham, the destination for that night, an arduous twenty-five miles of muddy road away.

Their intended route takes the company slightly to the west of the most direct route to London, since the lands around Grantham are part of the deceased queen's estate. The king has decreed that her tenants should be able to see her passing cortège, allowing them to pay their respects.

In order to allow progress to be as quick as possible, the king is not travelling with his full entourage of hundreds. Even so there are still a dozen horse-drawn carts carrying money, mattresses, curtains, clothing, food for the people and horses. There are armed knights, highly trained and ready to draw their swords to protect the king and his property at any moment, important royal officers, messengers, churchmen and servants of all kinds. Altogether there are about fifty people forming a ribbon that streams out behind the cart bearing the coffin. One of the king's messengers gallops ahead to the monastery of the Grantham Greyfriars so that preparations for the arrival of the cortège can be made.

Bunched together at the front of the procession is a small group of walkers close to the coffin itself, led by a priest bearing a cross. The coffin is covered by ornate cloths, pennants and valances of all colours, secured to a horse-drawn cart. Immediately following is a group of finely dressed men, the King of England with his most important courtiers and the Bishop of Lincoln. This group walks two abreast, keeping step, some carrying banners bearing the royal coats of arms.

After them comes a jumble of horses and carts, of servants, lesser priests and members of the king's household. The mood among the servants is sober, rain soaking their woollen clothing so that it lies damp and heavy on their shoulders. It is close to the shortest day of the year, and they are aware that the light will fail them early and, while reluctant to walk any faster, are hopeful of covering as much distance as possible while there is still visibility.

As they trudge along, some of the servants grumble among themselves that their rough garments rub against their skin, that their ill-fitting shoes make each step painful. They hope that they cannot be overheard, only to be reprimanded by one of their superiors, told sharply that they should be showing gratitude, not airing grievances. It is sinful, they are reminded, to envy the fine clothing of the grand people as it is to them that they owe their livelihood. In spite of the hardships, they should realise that though humble servants, they are fortunate in being able to expect sufficient food. And in having a pair of shoes they are better off than many of the king's poorer subjects. The servants of the king work hard but the rewards are good. Indeed, many of the people in the communities who observe them as they walk by look on enviously, left to eke out their meagre resources that bleak December.

Wherever they pass, through towns and villages, the king's subjects, whether smiths, wheelwrights, weavers or carpenters, stop in reverence and respect, transfixed, silently absorbing the news of the death of their queen. Many stand in awe, hardly able to comprehend the mortality of a monarch. Some passers-by interrupt their own journeys to swell the numbers at the back of the procession. While a few ask for alms, most are simply curious to know what it is that they are witness to, what great event they are sharing in. Many are overwhelmed on hearing that this is a royal entourage and fall down in prayer, hopeful that their lives will be lifted by this brief proximity to royalty, touched by its magic. Some try to place their feet on the ground where the king has walked, believing that by touching the hallowed ground that he has stepped upon some of his holy spirit will pass through to them and bring good fortune.

Edward understands the importance that he, as king, is seen by these common people and of meeting their lords, the knights of the shires. His many journeys throughout his realm are of so much more purpose than moving from place to place, they are spectacles that affirm his position of authority over the kingdom, reinforcing the bonds that tie the people. In taking his rule to his subjects he receives their loyalty in return. And as good fortune would have it, he looks every part the king, at least a head taller than most around him, easily distinguishable, awe inspiring.

Even the most disgruntled of the stable boys is forced to accept that it is difficult to complain much when the grand people too are obviously enduring discomfort. And no one can help but be touched by the devotion of the king to his deceased queen. Although he is no longer a young man, his once thick black hair now greying, there would have been no shame in King Edward continuing on horseback. But with Eleanor gone he cannot contemplate such consideration for his own comfort. In reverence to her he insists on undertaking the journey on foot, indifferent to the pain in his feet which is so insignificant compared to her ordeal. The privation for the bishop is surely felt even more keenly. An old man nearly seventy years old, still obliged to make long and arduous journeys across the distances within his extensive diocese, he too is walking, while holding himself straight and bearing the crosier of his office.

After many miles of travel and with more to come before there will be any rest for the night, the party joins the route of the River Witham, its waters swollen with rain. It is now dark, the cold still more biting. The mud along the way makes boots heavy and clogs the cart wheels. At last, the weary party arrives at Grantham. The town has long been an important marketplace, at a fork in the Great North Road from London, where it branches off to reach the ports to the east. This road, known to the Romans as Ermine Street, had seen travellers pass for hundreds of years. There are many houses crowded around the main street, homes to perhaps a thousand people.

On arrival the cortège is greeted by the Franciscan friars in their grey hooded robes, their candles casting a welcome glow in the darkness. They lead the procession to the friary and the doors of the church are thrown open wide to receive the coffin, giving a brief glimpse into the sacred ground of its interior. So many candles are burning inside that the light seems to burst out, a beacon revealing a momentary vision of the kingdom of Heaven on earth. The knights dismount and bow their heads in respect as the coffin is carefully borne into the church. The doors are slammed shut behind it, as if it is being swallowed up, absorbed into the holiness of God's House. It remains there through the night, the first of many along the route to London, watched over by the priests while candles burn, keeping evil spirits at bay and reminiscent of the divine light of Christ upon the world.

The Greyfriars have not long been settled in Grantham, their church consecrated only earlier that year. Few of the other buildings are yet complete and there is little room to accommodate the guests. Lodgings can only be found for the king and his immediate circle in the friary, while some others of the more important travellers are accommodated in the castle. The lower servants will have to keep warm through the night as best they can and huddle together under the carts. They are grateful that at least the friars are able to provide them with plentiful hot food. Sleep for them is snatched and fitful.

It is still dark when the travellers prepare to set off again the next morning, time to rise marked by the bells of the friars' early morning prayers. The destination for the night is the town of Stamford, again a distance of more than twenty miles. All are hopeful that the road will be easier than the one they followed the previous day. The travellers can now join the Great North Road, with its raised surface lifting it clear of the waterlogged land to either side. They push on, hour after hour, through the flat country. Just a few hills break the horizon, the church towers of distant settlements silhouetted against the sky. At least progress is quicker now, cart wheels able to turn more smoothly, clattering over the bumpy stones without getting clogged with mud.

That night the resting place for the coffin is St Mary's Church in the town of Stamford. Its great west tower stands proud above the cluster of wooden dwellings, the beautiful painted statues of saints in the niches keeping watch over the townspeople. As he prays, King Edward can almost feel her presence, whispering to him to help her.

*

For the third day of the journey it is not possible to take the most direct route south, continuing along the Great North Road through Peterborough and Huntingdon. That direction is flooded by the rising of the Rivers Nene and Ouse, as frequently happens during the winter months and is particularly severe with the incessant rains of recent weeks. The route must strike out further to the west, through the forests of Northamptonshire, where the road is poor and often blocked by fallen branches that the laden carts have to be lifted over and adding many unwelcome miles to the already long journey.

The destination for the night, the third since leaving Lincoln, is the village of Geddington. The settlement is chosen as it is the location of a royal hunting lodge that was built by Edward's grandfather, King John, and was a much favoured residence of King Edward and Queen Eleanor. The king and queen, like King John, took great delight in hunting in Rockingham Forest, often at this same time of year. They were always hopeful of, though never successful in, catching a wild boar as Edward's forebear had done. How acutely the king wishes that Eleanor were beside him now and that they could resume their hunt.

The village also has the benefit of a solid stone bridge. Built by King John, this structure replaced a flimsy wooden bridge that was frequently washed away, allowing him to reach his lodge without difficulty. The bridge was substantial, of large worked blocks that could defy the elements, wide enough to allow two carts to pass side by side. Though built for the convenience of a king, its presence is of great advantage to the ordinary people, allowing villagers to take their produce to market all year round and encouraging many travellers to cross here, bringing welcome trade.

That day in the village the rain has been relentless and the ground is awash with mud as the people and animals churned it up, the brief spells of sunshine inadequate to dry out the slippery mess. In nearby villages many people have lost their homes, helpless as they watched them being reduced to flimsy fragments of wood and straw, to be washed away by the roaring currents of the River Ise. Among these flat lands, the people of Geddington are able to make use of a hill close to the river where their huts can be built, safe from being swept away. Their dwellings, about thirty of them, are built in the shadow of the church which stands solidly on the hilltop as if its stone structure was the flowering of the ground beneath it, a great source of pride for the community.

Word reaches the village that the cortège is on its way and in spite of the lateness of the hour all the people except for sleeping infants come out to greet it. It is completely dark when the procession at last starts clanking discordantly over the bridge, its arrival announced by the church bells ringing a continuous, mournful peal. The shapes of the horses, riders and men on foot emerge out of the blackness of the evening, heralded by the sounds of voices and creaking of the carts.

The community stands in respectful silence, ignoring the chilly evening air, some holding candles. Many have witnessed the arrival of the king before on his visits to his hunting lodge with the queen accompanying him. Always to be so close to royalty, almost within touching distance, is thrilling, even terrifying. There are many sufferers from the distressing disease of scrofula, known as the King's Evil, with their painful and swollen necks. They know of the magical powers of the Royal Touch to cure the disease, yet none dares approach him.

The villagers soon realise that this arrival is of more significance than a royal hunting party and that they are witness to a unique occasion. It is just possible to pick out the unforgiving, angular shape of a coffin in the darkness. Word rapidly goes around the village that the queen is dead, a chilling reminder of human mortality, from which even royalty cannot be spared. The form of the king himself stands out in the gloom, his imposing stature making the others in the party look like boys.

The next day the cortège prepares for the twenty-mile journey to Hardingstone and the community of nuns at the Abbey of Delapré. Unable to stay in this establishment of women, Edward entrusts the coffin of Eleanor to the safekeeping of the sisters. On saying his prayers he leaves for his first night apart from Eleanor to stay at the royal quarters of Northampton Castle. The pain he feels at tearing himself away from the coffin and entrusting it to the care of others is almost physical. There is some reassurance that under the supervision of the abbess, Margery de Wolaston, he can be certain that prayers will be said through the night.

Bishop Sutton speaks warmly of Abbess Margery's abilities and the strength of her faith. She was chosen by the nuns to succeed the previous abbess who died eight years ago. In the first instance the bishop blocked her appointment, concerned that Margery, then just twenty, was too young to take on such responsibility. Only when he met her and questioned her carefully about her knowledge of the scriptures was he convinced that she was indeed the right choice for abbess. Since becoming abbess Margery met Queen Eleanor on the occasions of her many visits. The king must now entrust Eleanor to her care, hoping that her personal affection for Eleanor will magnify the power of her prayers.

From Delapré Abbey the king hopes to reach Woburn Abbey in Bedfordshire the next day but the distance of twenty-five miles in this season of short days proves too much. The party is therefore obliged to make an unplanned stop at the town of Stony Stratford, a settlement on a crossing place of the River Ouse, a mere thirteen and a half miles away. That night is again uncomfortable for many of the retinue, there being insufficient room to accommodate everybody under shelter. The river is often so high at this time of year that it is impassable. The next morning the king, anxious to waste no more time, makes the decision to risk the ford, although the waters run deep and look perilously dark. The horses go first to test the crossing and succeed in getting over safely. The king orders the strongest knights to follow, holding the coffin high above their shoulders. The watching retinue holds its breath until the body of the queen is safely delivered to the southern bank of the river.

The sixth night of the journey is spent at Woburn Abbey where the hospitality of the monks provides comfort. The procession then winds its way to Dunstable Abbey, where the Great North Road crosses the ancient track of the Icknield Way. At Dunstable Abbey the king prays at the shrine of St Fremund. Fremund was, like Edward, a great warrior and Edward is desperate to appeal to him, imploring him to work one of his miracles to save the queen from further suffering.

From Dunstable it is a distance of nearly fifteen miles to the Abbey of St Albans, the richest abbey in England that has for centuries been a centre for scholarship, a truly worthy resting place for Queen Eleanor's coffin.

The king spends some time visiting its magnificent library where the works of generations are preserved. He reads again the account of the life of his father, King Henry III, by Matthew Paris, the scholarly monk who died in 1259. Edward is saddened that Abbot Roger, who died earlier that year, cannot be there to receive the cortège. Roger knew Eleanor well from their many visits and the king regrets not being able to share memories of her with him.

*

That night the coffin lies alongside the shrine of St Alban. As King Edward prays for the soul of Eleanor, he tries to grasp some flecks of dust from Alban's tomb, as so many pilgrims have done before, he and Eleanor among them. This place has particular resonance for Edward as one to which he chose to bring Eleanor shortly after her arrival in England.

The story of Alban and the reasons for his significance were well known to Edward and Eleanor through the account by Matthew Paris. He wrote that around the year 300, during the time when Christians were persecuted for their faith, Alban was a humble soldier in the Roman army, stationed in the camp of Verulamium. Alban gave shelter to a Christian priest named Amphibalus, who was being pursued by Roman guardsmen. While in hiding Amphibalus converted Alban to the Christian faith and, when soldiers arrived at his door, he allowed Amphibalus to escape. But Alban's bravery was in vain as Amphibalus was soon caught and tortured to death. As punishment Alban was condemned to death by beheading, but before the sentence was carried out a miracle took place. On his way to his execution, Alban had to cross a river. In order that he could walk to his death on dry land, the waters parted for him. The executioner was overcome by the wonder of what he saw and fell to his knees, declaring himself a convert to Christianity. He refused to carry out the task of executing Alban. A replacement executioner was soon found, thus giving Alban the distinction of being England's first Christian martyr. As punishment for his sin, the eyes of the executioner instantly fell from their sockets. The man who refused to kill Alban was also put to death, thereby becoming England's second Christian martyr.

Alban was buried on the hill top close to the place of his execution and in time a chapel was built there. Many pilgrims visited and numerous miracles reported. In the year 793 the Saxon King Offa founded an impressive monastery to replace the simple chapel in recognition of the saint's greatness. A thriving town soon grew up around it, with many merchants wishing to sell their wares to the pilgrim visitors.

The town of St Albans was later beset by troubled times, the target of invasion by people from Scandinavia. The bones of Alban were moved many times for their safekeeping. On one occasion in around

990, the alarm was raised signalling an imminent Danish invasion. The abbot took the precaution of hiding the relics of Alban. He took the further safeguard of sending a false set of relics to the monastery at Ely, giving the monks there to understand that they were indeed receiving the genuine bones of the saint. The expected invasion did not take place and a deputation of monks from St Albans was sent to Ely to recover the bones. At first the monks of Ely refused to let them go. They finally agreed to return the relics but craftily sent back yet another set, keeping those that they believed to be the true ones. The genuine relics were eventually revealed under the altar in the abbey of St Albans where they had been all along. Over the years, amidst all the disruption of those troubled times, the exact location of Alban's original burial place was forgotten. It was eventually revealed in 1257 and elaborate shrines of Alban and Amphibalus were built to house their remains.

As he prays Edward puts some of the sacred dust in his pouch so that he can take some of the essence of this important English saint with him, a saint in Heaven with such power as to give assistance to Eleanor.

*

From St Albans the road ahead is difficult. The eighteen-mile onward journey to the Abbey of Waltham is through thick woodland, much of it hindered by fallen branches. As the travellers near their destination they cross the Great North Road, the route they would have been following had conditions been more favourable.

The king is tired and footsore but cannot stop himself imagining the pain of his queen on her journey through Purgatory, making the inconvenience of his own journey insignificant. In order to reach the abbey they have to cross the River Lea at the causeway. At this time of year its waters are swollen by rain, the rapid currents and uneven river bed making the task of the coffin bearers treacherous.

The coffin is received by the monks of Waltham Abbey who bear it through the great west door into their vast, cathedral-like church, its two massive central towers rising to a height of 400 feet, surpassing any other building for miles around. Edward prays, now alone, at the holiest, eastern, end of the abbey. He recollects so clearly the occasions that Eleanor was kneeling here beside him, with images of her torture pounding in his head. He prays to the sacred Holy Cross, as they so often did together. The remarkable story of the discovery of this modest-looking black flint cross was one he told to Eleanor so many years ago when he first brought her here.

The cross was found a hundred and fifty miles away in the village of Montacute, near Yeovil in the West Country around the year of 1020 when England was under the rule of the Danish king, Cnut. At that time the village blacksmith dreamed that God ordered him to tell the village priest to gather the villagers together, prepare them by prayer and fasting and lead them to the top of a nearby hill, where they were to dig for a buried cross. The incredulous blacksmith did nothing. When the dream recurred the next night he still did nothing. On the third night a figure appeared before him and seized his arm, leaving deep fingernail scratches. The blacksmith ran in fright to the priest. The priest, convinced by the visible scratches on the man's arm, summoned all the villagers and led them in procession to the mound. They started digging and soon uncovered a large stone underneath which there was a cross, exquisitely carved with a figure of Christ, together with a book of Gospels. Under the right arm of the cross was a smaller crucifix and under the left, a bell.

Lord of the Manor, Tovi the Proud, ordered the discoveries to be carried down to the village churchyard. He decided that the smaller crucifix should remain in the church at Montacute while the large cross and book of Gospels were put on a wagon to which twelve red oxen and twelve white cows were harnessed. Uncertain where the finds should be taken, Tovi called out the names of the famous religious centres of Canterbury, Winchester, Glastonbury, London, Malmesbury and more, but, whether pushed or pulled, the wagon refused to move. At last Tovi remembered a little church that he had started to build at his hunting lodge at Waltham, deep in Epping Forest. The moment it was mentioned, the cart surged forwards of its own accord. Many of the villagers followed the cart on foot, those who suffered ailments being miraculously cured on the way. Sixty-six of the travellers stayed to devote the rest of their lives to the service of the Holy Cross and founded the town of Waltham Cross. The church grew to become a great abbey, the famous cross attracting pilgrims in great numbers. It is this very cross that the king now prays to.

*

From Waltham the king and his most trusted knights take their leave of the cortège in order to ride ahead to oversee the preparations for the funeral at Westminster Abbey. The procession, under the supervision of Bishop Sutton, continues along the Great North Road for the remaining fifteen miles to London. King Edward has deep regrets about this parting of the ways but cannot consider leaving the funeral preparations to others. Even his great capacities do not allow him to be in both places and, having spent so much time over recent days in the company of the bishop, he knows that he can rely upon him to watch over the coffin.

After nine days on the road the weary travellers approach the city of London, entering by Bishopsgate. They thread their way through the tangle of narrow streets towards St Paul's Cathedral, where the coffin is to rest that night. The enormous silhouette of the building looms out of the fading light, its soaring spire piercing the heavens. The scaffolding of the masons who are continuing to extend the structure even further to the east can be picked out. Even with the evidence of their labours it is hard to believe that this structure is the work of mere mortals. Its solidity and scale make the jumble of makeshift mud and timber dwellings that crowd against its exterior seem so flimsy that they could disappear with a puff of wind. The candlelight from within illuminates the vast round window over the western entrance, revealing patterns delineated with stone bars so intricate that they are reminiscent of the petals of a rose opening out to full flower. It does not seem possible that forms of such delicacy can be created from the solidity of stone.

Though late in the day, the interior of the cathedral is still thronged with people going about their transactions: market traders with their stalls selling goods, scriveners offering their writing services, cloth merchants using the measure of length carved into one of the pillars. While the business of the day unfolds people, children and animals jostle past, along the well-trodden path between the building's transepts, seeking the shortest routes to their homes across the city. The air crackles with the noise of deals being done, money changing hands. Only occasionally can the sound of prayer be heard as people show their devotion to the real treasures that are held there, the knife of Jesus Christ, some hair of St Mary Magdalene, a fragment of the skull of St Thomas Becket, even the hand of St John the Baptist.

The coffin bearers push their way in and slowly inch towards the great altar as people fall aside to let them pass. The thrumming motion of the crowd gradually slows with the realisation of the importance of the occasion. As the people come to understand the magnitude of what they are witness to, they fall to their knees in prayer. The raucous sounds of the marketplace are within minutes replaced with the low humming of many voices.

*

The next day the funeral procession conveys Eleanor's coffin to the chapel of St Mary Rounceval in the village of Charing, close to the final destination of Westminster. Here Edward is reunited with Eleanor's coffin for a final period of quiet reflection alone with her. The next day it will be taken for its lying in state at Westminster Abbey before the funeral itself on the following day, when there will be no possibility of privacy.

The Eleanor Crosses

It is in Charing that the royal mews is situated, a place very dear to Edward and Eleanor, where they could enjoy the privileges of their royal birth. The mews holds Edward's prized collection of birds of prey and the queen's exotic parrots, many offered as gifts from the royal families of other countries and the envy of royalty across Christendom.

The cages are arranged around a courtyard garden with an ornate bird bath and fountain topped with a bronze falcon in the centre. Of all the places the cortège has stopped, this is the one with the most personal associations, where the burden of her absence feels heaviest. Here is Eleanor's garden, the place she could enjoy as if it offered sanctuary from the harshness of the world. That winter's evening the pungent smell of the ivy, holly and bay, their evergreen leaves redolent of the fidelity they shared, mixes with the cold rain to taunt him with her absence. Out of the corner of his eye he can sense her presence, stepping out of the shadows towards him. He listens for her voice but can hear only the water, flowing from the mouths of the bronze leopard heads of the central fountain, and running through the channels that cross the garden. The constant flow of the water, the symbol of everlasting life, is mocking him in his grief now that Eleanor has been taken from him.

*

His thoughts take him back to just a few months earlier when they were here together to prepare for the marriage of Margaret, the third of their five daughters. Edward could not have known in those glorious summer days that the vine arbour offering welcome shade from the sun and a token of eternal life would grow again without Eleanor. The smell then was sweet with roses intertwined with columbine, the flowers of the Virgin Mary and the Holy Ghost. The colourful flowers of her native Castile that she loved so much, hollyhock, wallflower and lavender, supplemented the native blooms carefully tended by the gardeners she brought to England. The future then seemed to hold such promise that he feels raw with the pain of finding himself here alone.

That night, with Eleanor's companionship snatched from him, Edward has no time for his treasured birds. His prized gerfalcons are here, sent by the King of Norway as tokens of friendship on the occasion of the betrothal of his daughter, the maid Margaret, to Edward's son, Prince Edward of Caernarvon. These beautiful birds now seem trivial, unable to reach him in his misery.

He returns to the church for this last time alone with Eleanor's body, determined not to leave her. There will be no sleep that night even though his chambers in the Palace of Westminster are a short distance away. It is hard to accept that Eleanor has already been gone for more than two full weeks, with her presence still so vivid to him. He cannot keep the terrible images of her suffering in Purgatory from his mind, knowing that while he has experienced hardship during the journey south she has been in constant torment. His despair is made worse by the knowledge that in Purgatory time is measured in much longer stretches than the equal time on earth. He feels helpless beside her body. He prays to all the saints in Heaven for surely among them there is one who can help the onward passage of her soul and give him guidance on how he can fulfil his promises and release her from Purgatory.

Even though there is comfort in the promise of being reunited in Heaven after the brief time on earth is over, the anguish at spending the rest of his mortal life without Eleanor weighs heavy. He cannot imagine the burden lightening. Yet his grief is nothing compared to the thought of her suffering. He prays as hard as he has ever prayed for the salvation of her soul, feeling that his words are disappearing unheard into the black night. Still he prays on, desperate for guidance on how to protect the woman he loves now she is dead. He is deeply perturbed by the fears Eleanor expressed during those final hours and mindful of his promise to her to do his utmost to ensure the offering of many prayers and Masses for her soul for ever more.

THE ELEANOR CROSSES

It is certain that no one, whether queen or commoner, can escape the hardships of Purgatory before they are permitted take their place in Heaven. This mighty king with all his immense resources, who can build castles, moving rivers at his command, is daunted by the power of the afterlife.

*

Once day has fully broken the funeral cortège gathers for the last time to transfer the coffin to Westminster Abbey for the lying in state. All who have been involved, whether noble or servant, are aware of having been part of something momentous. Though few knew Eleanor personally, the twelve days they spent together linked them in honouring their queen and what she signified. All understand that though of flesh and blood the king and queen are of different clay from ordinary mortals, especially chosen by God to protect the people. Their participation in the cortège surely brought them closer to God, touching them with the aura surrounding the monarch. Although distracted by grief and exhausted from his night without sleep, the king shows his appreciation to all the servants with a generous payment in recognition of their perseverance and loyalty over the long journey.

3.

REACHING WESTMINSTER

The coffin is lifted carefully onto a cart and hung with richly woven cloth, decorated with the coats of arms of the queen, those of England, León, Castile and Ponthieu and slowly makes its way towards the abbey. It is placed beside the great altar, close to the shrine of Edward the Confessor.

Behind the altar is a wonderful painted panel, inset with jewels and precious metals that glitter in the candlelight, gold, silver, copper and, most valuable of all, lapis lazuli that could only have been brought from the mountains of Afghanistan, thousands of miles away. In its centre Christ, as saviour of the world, is depicted holding an exquisitely detailed globe in his hand. Edward cannot now comprehend why the son of God did not see fit to save Eleanor, anger sharpening his grief.

Set in front of the altar is a pavement of astonishing beauty, gifted by the pope himself. It is made up of an intricate pattern of thousands of coloured stones, laid by highly skilled craftsmen brought from Italy for its construction. The stones, purple porphyry, green jasper, yellow marble, stone of pink, black, blue, used in the great buildings of Imperial Rome, allude to the richness of God's earth. Together they form a masterpiece, a vast, circular disc of veined alabaster, a shimmering white pool of near perfection at its centre surrounded by an intricate web of patterns, shapes within shapes, circles linked by spirals, parts forming a harmonious whole, laws of symmetry imposing rationality onto confusion. The square of the whole suggests the four elements, the four seasons, the four humours of the body, the four corners of the world, while the circle refers to perfection, to continuity. Within could be found any number of geometric shapes, the five pointed stars suggesting the five senses and the five wounds of Christ, while triangles refer to the Holy Trinity, the passage of the soul through time with the beginning, middle and end. Its labyrinthine complexity is a reminder of the tortuous journey that man faces to reach Heaven, the journey that Eleanor is now embarking upon as the coffin containing her body rests upon it.

The shrine of St Edward is the jewel at the heart of this magnificent abbey. It is carved from marble of the highest quality, brought from Italy, inlaid with precious stones of many colours, rich with jewels and enamels. In its base are seven recesses into which sufferers from scrofula crawl so the enduring power of the Royal Touch will give them deliverance from their affliction. The power emanating from the bones of St Edward will now help in relieving Eleanor's pain.

The next morning, 17 December, the lords are assembling in the abbey to make their farewells to the queen. All the lords of the realm are required to attend. Bishop Sutton, who has so devotedly attended the queen during her final hours and remained with the coffin since leaving Lincoln, is present to officiate.

As he greets the nobles King Edward is aware of the weighty symbolic importance of Westminster Abbey to the monarchy, a rightful place for the funeral of Eleanor, the place where he was christened and where he too will be buried when his time comes. It was in The Confessor's chapel that King Henry III, Edward's father, declared his wish to be buried, the place he intended to be a future mausoleum for the Plantagenet dynasty. King Henry had great faith in the power of Edward the Confessor, the only English king to be sanctified for the miraculous cures that he affected both in life and in death. Called Confessor for his great devotion to Christ without martyrdom, his saintly status was proved when his body was found uncorrupted on the opening of his tomb over one hundred years previously, with his joints still flexible and his features still brilliantly white.

Henry named his first born son after him and did much to honour him. The presence of his tomb in this royal burial place would offer protection to sovereign souls on their journey and for ever more. This at least must give some comfort to Edward.

*

Now, on this occasion of Eleanor's funeral, Edward listens to the prayers for the departed soul of his queen. The whole chapel is resplendent with colour and ornament, a feast for the eyes. The spaces above the arcade are thick with a repeated pattern of carved roses, each flower individually painted and adding to the richness of the total effect. Above, there are two tiers of windows, the painted glass glowing, creating tapestries of light. Even at this darkest time of the year the rays of sunshine through the lights of the glass create coloured patterns that dance on the stone flagstones, the spirit of God shedding his light on the world. Enclosing the whole, the vaulted ceiling is a vision of Heaven on earth, painted blue and gold and studded with jewels. The grandeur of the ceremony has not been seen before, forty-nine candles burning for each of her forty-nine years.

Edward is reminded of the many state occasions that he and Eleanor attended together and the many visits for their own personal devotions. Together they shared in the veneration of the sacred relics, the phial of the blood of Christ, part of the manger, some frankincense offered by the Magi, the Virgin's girdle that Eleanor herself used in childbirth. So many memories of their intertwined lives crowd his tormented mind.

The funeral ceremony is followed by a magnificent feast with meat in plenty, fine wines and exotic fruits. Alms are given to the poor who arrive in huge numbers, dirty, diseased people, holding out their hands for coins. A few try to push their way forward to receive the offerings but most wait in respectful silence, aware of the gravity of the occasion. Edward gives generously, knowing that an act of charity on Eleanor's behalf will assist the passage of her soul through Purgatory.

After the ceremony and funeral banquet at Westminster an array of clergy and dignitaries assembles for one final journey, processing towards the City of London, past the Palace of Savoy and other grand houses. The clattering of the city stops briefly as the king and his entourage pass by, no coffin now, just the small container holding the heart of the queen. They make their way towards the priory of the Blackfriars in the City of London where Eleanor has already built a chapel in readiness to receive her heart, the part of her that held the essence of her piety. Her choice for its burial place indicates the deep affection that she held for the Dominican order of friars, distinguished by their black robes, founded by St Dominic from her native Castile.

In solemn ceremony Eleanor's heart is placed in the small container that holds that of their sadly missed son, Alphonso, who died six years before, just ten years old and at that time the heir to Edward's throne. The monks of the Blackfriars are entrusted with watching over these precious remains.

*

Now that Eleanor has been buried, Edward is more acutely aware of her absence than ever. The space she has left is a void that weighs on him so heavily that it is like a presence in itself. He returns that night to his palace at Westminster to prepare for yet another departure. He intends to set out the following morning for the two-day journey to Ashridge in Hertfordshire and the palace of his cousin, Edmund, Earl of Cornwall. It is here that the king has decided that the court will spend this first Christmas without the queen at its head. In no mood for lavish celebration so soon after Eleanor's passing, he craves some time away from Westminster with his memories. Ashridge Palace is not large enough to hold the whole entourage but rooms can be found in the nearby village of Pitstone for him and the closest of his advisers, away from the trivial gossip and intrigue of the court.

Edward is grateful for the company of his cousin after the funeral as they ride together, someone with whom he can share memories of Eleanor. The king holds Edmund in high regard, an ally who has on many occasions shown loyalty to the crown by lending much needed money. It is thanks to his wealth that the king was able to implement the recall and reissue of the coinage of the realm in 1279 when its value became degraded through years of clipping for its metal. And it was Edmund to whom he entrusted the custody of the kingdom when he and Eleanor were required to spend time in France that same year.

Edmund does what he can to offer Edward solace at the loss of Eleanor, reminding him how he was blessed by having so many years of happiness with her. He himself was not so fortunate in the choice of wife made for him, having an acrimonious relationship with his own spouse, Margaret de Claire. Rather than seeking companionship, he has long refused to share a house with her, thus provoking the anger of Archbishop Pecham who took the extreme step of excommunicating him as punishment. Edward was indeed blessed that his relations with his wife had been so much more than duty, that he also felt a deep love for her.

As they ride together Edward falls silent for much of the time, barely noticing the changing scene as they pass by, his mind wandering back to his and Eleanor's times together and his thoughts of how he will mark her passing.

When the court assembles at the Palace of Ashridge Edward is joined by his children, Mary, Elizabeth and Edward, so young at eleven, eight and six to have lost their mother. He takes particular pleasure in the presence of Mary who took the veil at the priory of Amesbury five years before. He now deeply regrets his decision to allow Mary, at the age of six years, to take holy vows. Although he and Eleanor visited her five times since then and she was released to attend important court occasions, she was greatly missed by him and her mother.

THE ELEANOR CROSSES

That Christmas King Edward's fondness for his children gives him some small comfort. In particular, Elizabeth's resemblance to her mother reassures him that Eleanor's physical appearance at least continues through her children. His daughters try to distract him with suggestions of playing chess, but he cannot find any enthusiasm for the game. The beautiful jasper and crystal chess set that he gave to Eleanor just two Christmases ago when in Gascony remains unused.

For all the efforts of his family and courtiers, Edward is alone in grief. Lavish Christmas celebrations continue around him. But he has no appetite for the elaborate dishes, roasted swan, fine dry wines from Gascony, pomegranates, raisins, oranges and lemons from Eleanor's homeland of Castile which they used to enjoy so much. There can be no pleasure in delicious foods while Eleanor may at that very moment going through the tortures of starvation or worse. His patience exhausted with the shallow pleasures of feasting, he takes his leave.

*

That Christmas night, instead of taking part in the festivities, Edward returns to the church of Ashridge Priory where the whole company attended Mass earlier in the day. He kneels before the sacred shrine containing a phial of drops of blood from Christ's wounds as he suffered on the cross. This priceless relic was brought back by his cousin Edmund from his travels in Germany and was once in the possession of the heroic Holy Roman Emperor, Charlemagne. Edward prays long and hard.

At last, as day begins to dawn, he feels some lifting of the desperation that has haunted him. Perhaps his prayers have been heard, perhaps there is a way to reach his queen. In his mind, so active even while fogged with tiredness, he can hear Eleanor's voice whispering to him the names of the stopping places of the cortège. Those names, Lincoln, Grantham, Stamford, Geddington, Delapré,

Stony Stratford, Woburn, Dunstable, Waltham, St Albans, the city of London and Charing: places so different from each other, but now inextricably linked, echoing in his head.

In his mind's eye Edward sees the route carved out through his kingdom in front of him, a wavering line through the country with a curve bowing out to the west, large numbers of his subjects within its reach. As he reflects further on the journey and its twelve stopping places he is reminded of how touched he was by the respect given by the ordinary people of his kingdom as they realised they were witnesses to the passing of a queen. Many had taken time from their daily tasks to kneel in prayer, powerful enough, surely, to be heard by God. There must, he thinks, be a way to harness that power for ever more, to save the soul of his beloved Eleanor from the torture of Purgatory. While it is only the few who travel or live in the cities and see the great cathedrals for themselves, how many more people could be reached by creating permanent memorials in each of the places the cortège stopped, physical reminders of that journey?

Edward envisages the creation of lasting monuments for Eleanor of unprecedented grandeur. He remembers the memorials that were created for the revered King Louis IX of France, his uncle by marriage, who had succumbed to illness on the crusade in which they both participated in 1270. The ten stopping places of that funeral cortège on its return to France were remembered with *montjoies*, delicately carved stone markers such as those used during the Holy Wars to indicate sites from where Jerusalem could be seen. This is Edward's opportunity to build similar memorials yet on a scale grander still than those constructed for the French king.

A lasting memorial in each of the resting places will encourage the offering of prayers for Eleanor for all time. Her coffin passing through the communities will become more than just a memory, to be talked about by one generation to the next. Stone monuments will serve to make a permanent statement, a lasting symbol of royalty and devotion. The memorials will be not just reminders of Eleanor, but signifiers of the greatness of monarchy itself, representations of Queen Eleanor as an exemplar for every queen. They will allow the memory of the reign of Edward and Eleanor to live on in perpetuity, the affection felt for them by their subjects continuing through their descendants.

This vision takes form in his imagination. He will create a series of memorials to surpass all those previously created for any English monarch, king or queen, raised on steps to be seen by all. The memorials to Eleanor will be a source of pride for each of the communities that receives one. The king will commission statues of his wife, several for each monument, to be placed high up, looking down on the people. The many viewpoints of her gaze will capture everything, a secular Virgin Mary. Though merely statues, the sense of being watched over by a queen will surely serve to provide inspiration for good behaviour and also compassion, as if the queen were herself a saint. The strength of the prayers of the people, clerical and lay alike, would surely encourage God to look down favourably at the royal family and fulfil Edward's promise to the dying Eleanor to make certain of the safe passage of her soul.

Perhaps the monuments will become meeting places for the people too, somewhere for small groups to gather. In communities where stone building is scarce, the steps of the memorials will provide a welcome place to sit, somewhere that will not turn to mud when it rains. As people go about their daily business the crosses will be places where they can share a collective memory of pride in their community, marked out as being the stopping place for the funeral cortège of a queen of England. Edward imagines the monuments becoming stages on a pilgrim route, twelve Stations of the Cross for Eleanor. He envisages the ribbon of crosses through the country providing a permanent link between the twelve disparate communities, reinforcing the unity of his kingdom.

Edward believes that by making their queen visible to his subjects he will harness the affection that is there for her, as consort to their king, the feminine and forgiving face of monarchy. He will create a groundswell of love for her, inviting prayers from the people of England.

Yet the crosses are to be much more than crude markers. Eleanor's monuments are to be lavish works of art, rich with elaborate decoration. The king envisages them to be truly masterful creations, exemplars of the skill of the best craftsmen. He imagines them becoming reminders of his and Eleanor's reign that will endure for generations. While the monuments will respect places where the queen's coffin rested overnight, each will be carefully positioned to be seen by as many travellers as possible, thus amplifying the prospective number of prayers for her.

In addition to reaching the ordinary people Edward will make sure that the burial places of Eleanor's actual physical remains are marked on an outstanding scale. She will have not just one tomb, but three, all the works of masters. As well as her burial place in that most prestigious of royal mausoleums, Westminster Abbey, there will be tombs of equal splendour for her heart at Blackfriars Priory and her viscera in the Angel Choir of Lincoln Cathedral. Although it is occasionally known for royalty to be provided with two tombs, to have three is unique. The choice of resting places for his queen alongside those of saints, St Hugh at Lincoln and Edward the Confessor at Westminster, is in itself a demonstration of the esteem in which Edward held Eleanor. Monarchy, exemplified by Queen Eleanor, will be inextricably associated with the sacred, an honour to be conferred upon Eleanor as queen consort and daughter of a king. In the chapels that hold her remains royalty and sanctity will be drawn together in the hearts and minds of the faithful.

Each of these three tombs will be of the highest standards of workmanship, bringing together the skills of the finest craftsmen, metal workers, goldsmiths and painters as well as sculptors. Provision will be made for candles to be kept burning around the tombs, their light drawing many towards their riches and inviting their prayers.

As well as the physical memorials to Eleanor, Edward will also put in place endowments for the celebration of Masses in remembrance of her in perpetuity, another means to protect her soul. There will also be provision of alms from her estate, in itself a good deed worthy of remission from Purgatory, while encouraging prayers of gratitude from those receiving them.

THE ELEANOR CROSSES

*

At last, the long night is at an end. Visions of stone monuments fill Edward's head as he imagines the sounds of the chanting of Masses while candles flicker. Perhaps the images and echoes in his head are the product of his confused, unrested mind, or perhaps his prayers have indeed been heard and the saints he has spoken to have given him their guidance.

He feels some solace in the realisation that the burials, however solemn, will not be the end. Indeed, they will be a beginning. At last, more than a month after Eleanor's death, he sees there is a way that he as king can use his powers to make sure that she is honoured always by their people.

4.

BUILDING A LEGACY

Edward's patience for the Christmas celebrations exhausted, he is anxious to get on with the business of Parliament to be held at Ashridge Priory so that he can announce his plans for the commemoration of Eleanor. When all are assembled Edward describes to his magnates the crosses that he plans to build, her tombs, the Masses and the giving of alms. The lords are incredulous at the breadth and ambition of what he is proposing. Concerns are inevitably raised about the cost of such an extensive project, but Edward is resolute in his decision. The lords are relieved by his pledge that it will be Eleanor's dower estates alone which fund the memorials and there will be no additional pressure on the public purse. The building of the monuments will truly be her legacy.

Edward returns to pray at Ashridge Priory. He prays ardently, hoping that Eleanor will be able to hear him and receive some comfort from the actions that he has now taken. Parliament over, his announcement made, it is only now that he can turn his attention again to the affairs of his country and to the unfinished business in Scotland.

Edward welcomes the diversion of starting the New Year with a flurry of activity, putting his vision for the commemoration of Eleanor into practice, to once again be initiating a building project as he has done with his castles in Wales. He enjoys working with masons, practical men who can make stone buildings emerge from the ground, taking satisfaction from harnessing their technical skills in the realisation of his grand concepts. In his mind's eye he sees beacons of stone standing on the roadways of England, inviting prayers for his Eleanor and channelling them towards Heaven. He is fiercely determined that they will be created without delay in order to spare her as much as possible from the pains of Purgatory. It is essential that no time will be lost at the start of the spring building season.

The royal master masons are called to the Palace of Westminster to plan the building of the crosses. In attendance are Richard of Crundale, his brother and assistant, Roger, John of Battle and Michael of Canterbury. All the masons are men with many years of experience, having worked long apprenticeships where they learned their trade. Also in attendance are the renowned sculptors, William of Ireland and Alexander of Abingdon, similarly stonemasons by training who now specialise in creating images of the human form to grace important buildings. These men whom the king calls upon to realise his plan are indeed masters of their craft.

The most distinguished of the masons is Richard of Crundale who has been Chief Mason for London Works for over ten years and has served the king well. He worked his apprenticeship at the Tower of London under Master John of Acre who returned with the king from the Holy Land in 1274. He later went on to work for the king at Westminster Abbey where he is now in charge of the busy workshop.

Edward impresses upon the masons the urgency and significance of this new project. Twelve monuments of the complexity he envisages will require considerable resources and will take several years to complete. Master Richard, familiar with the impatience of the king, has some concerns that it will not be possible for a building team to complete more than one monument before building programmes are shut down for the year at the 1 November festival of All Saints. But Edward is driven by his need to protect Eleanor.

The masons are all impressed by the ambition of Edward's project and daunted but know of his achievements as a great builder of castles, especially in Wales, shifting men and materials in a matter of months to create immense structures. All are familiar with his insistence on high standards that, on this most personal of projects where beauty as well as practicality are key, will be more rigorous than ever. Some have been witness to his formidable outbursts of temper. There are even rumours that he once frightened a man to death, a story that is surely not to be believed. Yet for all his impatience, they know the king to be fair, a message that they communicate to the teams who work under them, and that he pays generous rewards when satisfied. He will, even though lord of the realm, apologise when he recognises his anger to be misplaced. It is no secret that he paid recompense to an esquire he attacked with a stick in an outburst of temper earlier that year.

The king describes in some detail his concept to the craftsmen. Each monument is to be constructed in four tiers. The first, reaching to a height of six feet, is to be adorned with the arms of Queen Eleanor, the heraldic shields displaying the castle of Castile, the lion of León, the diagonal lines representing Ponthieu and the lions of England. Above that is to be set a series of niches, suitable housing for statues of the queen, standing three feet in height. Above that is to be an ornamental stage, the crowning glory for the statuary, a further two feet high. Each monument is to be surmounted by a cross. The two London crosses are to be even more elaborate, embellished with gilding and inlay, in recognition of the large numbers of people they will be seen by.

'It is agreed that labour will be concentrated in a few places, with enough men employed that within a matter of months a number of the monuments will be complete. They decide upon a building programme using four teams of masons, each working under the most accomplished master masons in the land. Work will begin promptly at the beginning of the building season after the Easter observances, commencing with Lincoln, Grantham, Stamford and Cheapside.

Master Richard and the other master masons are perplexed by the king's plans for a series of monuments on such a scale, having never built anything of this sort. But they know better than to question his instructions, aware that once he has a mind to do something it is not changeable. They feel admiration for the devotion the king is showing to his consort, aware that there must be many matters of state demanding his attention. Most of them are familiar with the king's working methods from previous royal commissions. They know that although he will stipulate overall design, they will be allowed to use their own artistic sensibility and pride in workmanship to enhance the whole. This is their chance to experiment with shape and pattern in carving on a small scale, without having to give consideration to blending in with an existing building. Here is an opportunity to create a unique structure that is of a piece, to be appreciated visually as an integrated whole, small but complete. They are excited by this new challenge, eager to use their skills to the king's satisfaction, although not a little anxious about the time allotted them.

John of Battle is dispatched to Stamford while the Crundale brothers are instructed to go to Grantham. Richard of Crundale, as the most senior and well-respected of the masons is also tasked with meeting with Richard of Stow to pass on instructions for the building of the cross at St Katherine's Priory in Lincoln at which Eleanor's body was embalmed. Master Richard is then engaged on decorative carving for the Angel Choir of Lincoln Cathedral and not on this occasion required to travel the long distance to Westminster to meet with the king personally.

Although the Crundale brothers are glad to be involved at the inception of this project to which the king obviously attaches such importance they are unenthusiastic about the prospect of a building season in Grantham, and are even unsure where it is. They feel they are deserving of the commission of the most impressive of the monuments to be built in the forthcoming season, the Cheapside Cross, at the heart of the city of London.

This commission carries great prestige, surpassing the others in significance. The king allocates generous funds for the completion of this monument that will be seen by so many people in the heart of the city, more than double the sums allowed for the other crosses. But instructions for that monument are given to Master Michael of Canterbury. The other masons know better than to express their resentment that a mason who has not previously been in the king's service is entrusted with this commission. But Edward was much impressed by his work at The Prior House near the Cheapside Church of St Mary-le-Bow and has fixed upon giving him this opportunity.

When the masons depart having been given their instructions Edward feels something of a sense of release, his yearning for Eleanor channelled into the realisation of a worthy legacy for her. The masons have now been given their challenge to deliver his vision.

The master masons tasked with the construction of the crosses spend the short days of February planning how they will accomplish the tasks they have been given. Although all are confident of the skills of the teams they can draw upon, there is a particular sense of expectation around this project. Neither time nor quality can be compromised. It is fortuitous that the task of purchasing and transporting materials for the construction of the crosses will be manageable, those parts of the country being rich in stone.

Master Richard sends orders to the quarry at Ancaster, conveniently situated between Lincoln and Grantham, for deliveries of stone to both towns, the three places linked by the Great North Road. There is a permanent mason's workshop in Lincoln, adjacent to the cathedral, where the stone can be received and held in readiness for the arrival of the masons. The delivery to Grantham is of greater concern. It will be best for its arrival to be planned as soon as possible after the masons, to ensure its safe keeping without delaying building work. If materials are delivered too soon they are in danger of damage or theft, too late and the workmen will have to be paid when not fully engaged with work.

John of Battle, instructed to build the cross at Stamford, can draw upon the quarry only a short distance away at Barnack. It is close enough that he plans to go there in person to select the stone once he arrives at Stamford with his team. To do so will be of great benefit as Barnack stone can show significant differences, with its various shades of pink, flecked with darker swirls of pattern and his choice of material will be important for the appearance of the final work. The stone at Ancaster, though of good quality, is more uniformly grey in colour.

The Crundale brothers, Richard and Roger, make ready to set out from London for Grantham early, in advance of the traditional Easter time beginning of the construction season. They are aware that the journey will be longer and less comfortable by setting out before spring has truly arrived, possibly delayed by floods, but hope that good fortune will be with them so that work can start without delay. They are also at an advantage from having long been established in the city of London and are readily able to inform their team, giving them ample advanced notice of the plans and time to make their own preparations for the journey and make provision for their families.

The Crundales' status as royal master masons means that they can afford horses for themselves to ride and to pull the carts carrying provisions and equipment. The journeymen masons, five men they know to be skilled and efficient workers, will travel with them on foot, affording them all greater protection from attack on the most dangerous parts of their route. They will need more labourers for some of the heavier parts of the work which do not require the specialist training of the stone mason and are confident of being able to find willing workers when they reach their destination.

The journeymen masons, never guaranteed skilled masonry work in the springtime after the long winter break, for the most part welcome this opportunity. Even so, for many of them the departure is not without concerns, necessitating leaving their families to support themselves while they are away. Some journeymen are obliged to turn the work down, unable to leave their homes as their families are reliant on their weekly wage. For them there is no other way for their dependants to obtain money during the long months, no father or brothers to whom they can entrust their care.

*

The Crundales and their team reach Grantham in safety after ten weary days of travelling, the journey passing without undue incident. Although it is late in the day when they reach the settlement a number of townspeople meet them on arrival. Lodgings are soon found for Master Richard and Roger with the rich merchants of the town, the journeymen settling down to sleep as best they can until better arrangements are made.

At first light the masons start setting up their workshop, with workbenches of long planks set on trestles for laying out equipment, erecting woollen awnings to give some cover from the rain. More and more townspeople come to see what is happening, having heard word of their arrival, inquisitive to discover what is to be built. They listen with curiosity as the masons explain that this will be a monument for the departed Queen Eleanor. This being the first construction of its kind, they themselves have some difficulty explaining. It is only Master Richard who, having taken instruction from the king, has much grasp of what the completed cross is to look like.

Many of the people of Grantham saw the cortège when it stopped here the previous winter and paid their respects to the Queen of England, but could not have imagined that the events of that day are to be marked in this way. Their church, of course, holds tombs for those wealthy enough for such provision, places where their families could continue to offer prayers for the souls of the departed, but to create a memorial for one short stopping place of a coffin was something unknown. Even the priest, a learned man who has studied the written word of God, has never heard of such a construction.

The townspeople are given to understand by the masons that it is an honour that their town has been selected, in the first instance as a stopping place for the cortège and then for its permanent commemoration. For the most part they are most happy to give these craftsmen a warm welcome, glad to have visitors. The masons will have good wages, money which they will be spending on food and goods, on lodgings and generous amounts of ale.

Once the masons have been set to their tasks, knowing that there are several days of preparatory work to be done that does not require complex adjustment or measurement, Richard of Crundale leaves them under the supervision of his brother, Roger. Taking one of the unskilled workers with him for safety, he sets out on horseback for the day's journey to Lincoln. There he will meet Richard of Stow in order to communicate to him the instructions of the king for the building of the cross at St Katherine's. For the time being any further decorative enhancements to the Angel Choir of the cathedral where Richard of Stow has been employed will have to wait for the completion of what they have come to call the Eleanor Cross.

As work progresses, the Grantham townsfolk watch the monument rise day by day, wondering how much higher it will reach. First an octagonal platform on a series of nine deep stone steps is created upon which a tower of stone begins to appear. The tower seems to reach ever upwards in front of the eyes of the townsfolk. Soon it is above head height of even the tallest man. The workmen lash together long poles and planks to make a frame with platforms around the growing construction. Out of a shapeless pile of wood they have soon created a structure that is secure to work from. The platforms are reached by climbing up struts fastened with rope to the longest poles that can be found. The men seem completely lacking in fear as they shin up the poles, nimble, cat-like, even while using one hand to balance a block of stone on their shoulder.

More and more stone keeps arriving, roughly shaped thick blocks strapped to carts, the horses struggling under the weight. While the younger masons continue building the monument the more experienced masons, under the watchful eye of the master, work on the grey slabs at the workbench with small chisels using light taps of delicate precision. Out of the unwieldy stone, sharply defined heraldic shields emerge, standing in relief against a perfectly smooth background. These are set into position on the lower stages of the monument.

The structure soon dwarfs all other buildings in the town with the exception of the church. When it has reached the height of three tall men, there is a change in the formation, the structure becoming narrower. The blocks of stone are continued upwards, leading the eye towards Heaven, now leaving openings. Once this stage is prepared slender shafts of stone, which arrived from the quarry ready carved and polished, are cut to the right length by the master and lifted into position to frame them. This stone is particularly good quality, worth the expense of bringing by road and river from Purbeck, far away on the south coast of England. It is remarkable for the smooth polished surface that can be achieved, bringing out deep shades of purple, but has to be treated with great care as it can easily shatter. No one but the master is willing to take on the task of cutting the shafts, the others fearful of damaging them and the cost being deducted from their wages.

Master Richard explains that four spaces which have been created are niches to house statues of Queen Eleanor, figures that the king has especially ordered from the famous figure sculptor, William of Ireland. Master William and his team have been working hard throughout the winter to produce images of her, at least twenty in total for this and other crosses. Each one, after the rough shapes were hewn out, was shaped by the hand of the master, with the delicacy of the carving demanding his skill. When the figures arrive they are lifelike, remarkably matched, with a grace that sets them apart from common womanhood. The forms seemed to move with a slight sway, the heads gently inclined, a smile playing around the lips, encapsulating queenly benevolence. Her hair hangs loose, feminine and virginal. The statues are carefully painted in bright colours to draw the eye of the beholder, enticing them to offer prayers.

William of Ireland is to be paid £3/6/8, not in total but for each figure alone. For the journeymen, such sums are staggering, one statue being perhaps worth what they could expect to earn in a year, even though they are better off than many. Now a wealthy man, William of Ireland works at the sculpture workshop at Westminster Abbey where his services are always in demand for creating statuary. It is from here that the statues are sent, carefully wrapped in cloth and secured to carts for the journey, along the route that the coffin of Queen Eleanor followed and treated with nearly as much care.

Due to the preciousness of the statues, they are kept in the church where they can be locked at night for safekeeping, together with the valuable small tools that can easily be stolen, waiting to take their place in their permanent home. When the monument is nearly ready to receive the statues, Master Richard very slowly drills a hole into the base of each in preparation for fixing them into position. This task requires great concentration as one slip can cause the delicate sculptures to fracture.

Among their tools the masons have brought long metal spikes, sharpened to a point at one end. These are carried up to the niches and hammered into position, creating a peg for the sculptures. The brightly painted statues are now carefully hauled up to the wooden platform that has been formed beside them and lifted into place, the load lightened by the concealed hollowed back. The figures now firm, Eleanor can look down over the town in all directions, giving her blessing to those who pass, inviting prayers for her in return.

And still the stone tower continues higher, now narrowing more quickly, supporting small elaborate turrets to the sides, dripping with foliage-like carving. After the weeks of hard work the monument stands to the height of at least six men. Finally a simple stone cross with beautifully carved vines scrolling around the shaft is lifted to the very top by the strongest men, carrying it between them in a cradle of lashed rope. There is a moment when the careful control is lost and it swings suddenly, causing alarm among the masons that it might crash to the ground. But the ropes hold firm and it is soon brought into check. The cross is set in position, using a weight attached to a string to ensure that its alignment is true and secured by an upstanding wooden support tied to the lower stages of the monument. The support is left in place for several days while the mortar sets.

The memorial is now complete and the dismantling of the wooden structures around it seems to take place in no time at all. The masons pack up their equipment with practised efficiency, ready to depart leaving no trace of their presence. The long high street with its wooden huts and muddy pathway is now dignified with a stone structure over forty feet tall, its pinnacle demanding to be looked up at. Where all the structures around are plain it is thick with embellishments, its complexity inviting longer consideration. Its vivid colours stand out from the pervasive greyness, drawing the eye towards it. There is nothing nearby it can be compared with yet the monument looks as if it belongs, as if it was always meant to be there and there it means to stay, to be seen by people in their hundreds as they come to market.

Over the course of that building season two other crosses are completed, at Lincoln and Stamford. The cross at Lincoln is placed outside the city walls at the gates of St Katherine's where Eleanor's body started its journey, ensuring that it is seen by many travellers as they enter the city from the south. As at Grantham, the one at Stamford forms a marker on the busy high street. The cross at Cheapside, given its scale and complexity, is only completed to the half way stage, to be continued the following spring.

*

During the building season of 1291 the king is given positive reports by his inspectors dispatched across the realm to check on building works. Consequently the master masons in charge of the crosses are all assured of further work the following year. Richard of Crundale is given the prestigious task of carving the tomb at Westminster Abbey, delighted not only that his skills have been acknowledged but that he will not have to endure the journey away from home. John of Battle is to go to Dunstable to build a similar cross to the one he completed at Stamford while Michael of Canterbury is to finish the Cheapside Cross. Richard of Stow, builder of the Lincoln cross, is the only one not retained to continue with the projects for the commemoration of Eleanor. Instead he is to take charge of the building of a new cloister for Lincoln Cathedral, an undertaking to which the bishop has given his particular support. As a mark of thanks to Bishop Sutton for the compassion he showed the dying Eleanor and during the progress of the cortège, the king makes a personal donation to these works.

THE ELEANOR CROSSES

Easter of 1292, more than a year after Eleanor's death, is painful for the king, bringing with it the recollection of their household tradition by which Eleanor's maids would hold him to ransom until he gave each of them a sum of money. Only then, to their great amusement, was he permitted to re-join the queen in her bedchamber after the frustrations of the abstinence of Lent. This second Easter without her and still feeling her loss, he continues to mark the occasion by giving the maids their payment. At least now he has the relief of knowing that some of the crosses are complete, that the flow of prayers for her has begun and building work is about to recommence, bringing the assurance of more.

It is not just stonemasons with whom King Edward is working for his commemoration of Eleanor. Her tombs in Lincoln, Westminster Abbey and Blackfriars are to draw together the skills of the greatest goldsmiths, metal workers, painters and carpenters of the age, to be truly worthy of a queen.

For the two large tombs in Lincoln and Westminster he imagines glorious effigies resting on them, images of Queen Eleanor ready for judgement day. Not content with mere marble, always thought to be the stuff of prestigious effigies, he visualises figures in bronze, greater than life-size models inlaid with gold and burnished to perfection. Nothing of such ambition has ever been attempted before. While many small works in bronze are made at the workshops of Cheapside, small sculptures for the wealthy to give as gifts or souvenirs to sell to pilgrims visiting shrines of favoured saints, nothing of such magnitude has been previously attempted. Such effigies will set Eleanor's tombs apart from others, their shining brilliance drawing prayers to them. Their sheer richness will also confer prestige upon the English royal family.

As he makes his plans for Eleanor's effigy he considers also the tomb of his father, Henry III, in its place of honour in Westminster Abbey, opposite that of the much revered Edward the Confessor. Of King Henry's many building projects the one by which he set greatest store was the completion of Westminster Abbey, yet when he died the nave remained unfinished. Other pressing demands on Edward's resources have not allowed him to complete it. Edward prays that King Henry will consider honour to be satisfied by the addition to his tomb of a wonderful bronze effigy. He intends to commission a work that will reflect the greatness of their lineage, truly marking out the Plantagenet dynasty as golden and undoubtedly to be the envy of his French royal cousins.

The only craftsman who can possibly create works on such a scale is William Torel, the greatest goldsmith in England, indeed in Christendom, famous for being able to make metal malleable in a way that nobody else can achieve. Torel is summoned to the Palace of Westminster to discuss the project with the king. Although the work will occupy him and his workshop for several years and the cost of such a quantity of precious metal is immense, the king is undeterred. Torel is, of course, aware of the great practical difficulties of preventing the bronze from cracking when working on such a scale and does not hide them from the king. Nonetheless, he agrees to take on the challenge, flattered by being given such a prestigious commission.

Torel sets up a temporary workshop in the Abbot's cemetery at Westminster Abbey where there is sufficient space to allow him to work on the effigies. The first task is to model the three figures from clay at a size slightly larger than life. The process is particularly slow as the king is concerned to be involved, to ensure that a good likeness of the queen is achieved. Although the living Eleanor is lost to him he imagines being able to look on her image and be reminded of her as she was and for generations to come to look upon her and appreciate her beauty.

Once they have hardened sufficiently the three clay models are painstakingly covered with a thin, even layer of wax and the whole form enclosed in clay. Now the bronze is prepared. The metal bars are heated in a cauldron inside a kiln built for the purpose, with thick stone walls. The workmen are accustomed to working in great heat, but once the fires have been burning for many hours the heat from the oven is almost unbearable. The stone slab at its opening is pulled away to receive the vat of metal, the heat blasting out of its cavernous interior, surely a taste of the fires of Purgatory to come. When ready the pot of glistening, liquid metal is lifted out by four strong men, supported by wooden prongs.

The dangerous process of casting the metal cannot be delayed long before it starts to harden and become unworkable. The whole company holds its breath as the valuable bronze is poured through a clay funnel into the pipe at the top of each model in turn, causing the wax to melt and drip out of the hole at the bottom. The flow must be steady and even, to ensure that the figures are uniformly covered. It is essential not to waste any of the molten metal, such is the value of the bronze.

There is now nothing to be done but be patient before it can be seen whether the efforts of the goldsmiths will be successful. It will be some weeks before the metal will be completely hard, allowing the rough encasing of clay to be chipped away, time when the goldsmiths return to the making of small items for monasteries and households of the nobility.

When the time comes at last the process of removing the clay to reveal the hidden metal is painstaking and tense. Although William Torel and his assistants are impatient to see the figures in their entirety it is necessary to use gentle hammer blows as too much force could irrevocably damage the surface of the metal.

The figures are finally revealed and found to be flawless. It is astonishing that such lifelike figures are achievable in cold, unforgiving metal. Eleanor is presented in simple robes, her hair falling loosely about her shoulders. The flowing lines of her garments, their folds softly overlapping at her feet and curls of her hair capture a brief moment between movements. Her right hand is raised to hold a sceptre indicating her office, her left fingering the cord of her mantle. Even though the figure is destined to recline on a tomb slab, she is presented as a standing woman, forever a monarch, capturing a timeless image of an idealised queen. She is presented as if ready for the moment of coronation and of judgement day.

There is yet more life to be revealed from the metal. The figures are still black, their surfaces dull. The next task is to laboriously polish them in order to coax out the glorious reflective shine of the bronze. Once the surfaces are smoothed and shining, gilding of gold leaf is meticulously applied, the warmth of the colours belying the coldness of its touch, the brightness of the images certain to attract people to it. The untarnishable character of the bronze will ensure that its brilliance will persist, continuing to draw prayers for all time.

William Torel's effigy of Queen Eleanor (www.findagrave.com).

THE ELEANOR CROSSES

*

By the summer of 1293 the carved tomb chests are complete and William Torel's exquisite effigies are at last ready to be fixed in place. King Edward is delighted with the results. It is a simple task to carry the figures of Queen Eleanor and King Henry to their resting places in Westminster Abbey, but the task of transporting the effigy intended for the tomb in Lincoln Cathedral is considerable. It is shown nearly as much consideration as was the body of the queen herself, carefully wrapped in cloth to prevent damage. The most trusted team of the king's knights, swords at the ready, are charged with ensuring the safekeeping of this valuable piece on the ten-day journey to Lincoln. Once there, it will be securely fixed into position on the completed tomb chest, ready for its consecration.

The cross that the king considers the most important is the one at Charing, opposite the entrance to the royal mews, just a short distance from the Palace of Westminster. Of all the monuments this is the one that he himself will see most frequently and he intends it to surpass all the others in its elaborate splendour. For its completion the king allocates more than three times the sum allowed for the Cheapside Cross, seven times each of the others. For that investment he expects magnificence, carving in the best quality stone, inlaid jewels gilded with gold leaf. Great quantities of Purbeck marble are ordered from Corfe, to be brought to London by river, also stone of the highest quality from Caen, across the sea in Normandy. The monument is to be resplendent with colour and gilding, glittering in the sunlight.

The work is tasked to Richard of Crundale, master mason for the cross in Grantham and the tomb in Westminster. It is to begin in 1292, and be completed over two building seasons. The king takes a close, if impatient, interest in its progress, frequently visiting when resident at the Palace of Westminster, but he is greatly perturbed at the news he receives on his return from the war in Scotland in April 1293. A few weeks after recommencing building that spring, Master Richard suddenly collapsed while climbing the scaffolding to the third tier of the monument and fell to his death. The suddenness of his end was shocking to all present. Just moments before, he was working with his usual energy, performing the physical tasks of a much younger man. The masons heard him let out an abrupt, piercing cry of pain and turned to see him fall twenty feet to the ground. Denied the opportunity of a good death, it is as if he died twice over, no opportunity to atone for the sins of his lifetime which remained unsettled. A priest is summoned immediately and Mass offered for his soul as it is received into Purgatory.

The masons continue to work under the supervision of Master Richard's brother, Roger, but with some sense of disquiet among the team. They cannot understand why a good man, as they believe Master Richard was, should have been denied the opportunity to receive the sacraments of death. Fearing that the abruptness of his end is a sign of God's displeasure, perhaps of His dissatisfaction with their workmanship, they carry on hesitantly. For the building of the cross to be blighted with mortality in such a stark way, they fear will bring bad luck to them all.

The king comes to inspect progress soon after his arrival at Westminster Palace. All the masons are told to put down their tools while he addresses them. He speaks of the esteem in which he held Master Richard, and assures them of his conviction that his demise, though a personal tragedy, is not an expression of God's anger. He, as the anointed king, tells them that the construction of such a monument to his deceased queen unquestionably has God's blessing. They should feel it an honour to be involved in its creation and are justified in being proud of their workmanship.

Roger of Crundale, in particular, feels a surge of gratitude when the king promises them that he will remember Master Richard in his prayers, as the devotions of the king will undoubtedly carry great weight in assisting the passage of the soul of his brother on its onwards journey. He is also heartened that the king assures him of his confidence in his ability to take over the role of master mason. After the king's words the masons return to work with newfound enthusiasm, even more so when he stays for a while to work alongside them, pushing some heavy barrows of mortar. By the time King Edward returns to the palace the masons are determined to live up to his expectations, their pride in their work restored.

Master Roger does indeed finish the task that has been set him and the completed Charing Cross is truly splendid, sparkling like a precious jewel-encrusted reliquary of vast proportions. He is gratified that the king retains his services the following year.

At the outset of the 1293 building season Roger of Crundale is sent to work on the cross at Waltham where he is assisted by Dymenge de Reyns, the mason who carved Eleanor's tomb at Lincoln Cathedral. The cross itself is to be situated on the main road near the ford across the River Lea. It will be seen here by many more travellers than it would by the gates to the abbey a mile away where Eleanor's coffin rested.

While Master Roger and some of the skilled masons are given accommodation in the abbey guest rooms the journeymen set up camp by the site of the cross so that the materials and tools can be watched over. The monks keep them well provided with food and drink and tell them stories of the marvels of the abbey's most sacred possession, the mysterious Holy Cross, that make them fear and wonder at its power in equal measures.

One such tale was of the miracle that saved the life of a young man named Matheus, more than a hundred years before. He had an agonising ulcer on his right foot that was spreading up his leg. His mother, beside herself with worry, went to the church of Waltham Abbey and prayed to the Holy Cross through the night for her son's life. Meanwhile the figure of Christ appeared to Matheus as he slept and asked him if he would promise to obey God and live a good life.

The desperate Matheus swore that he would. The shadowy Christ then seized hold of the poisoned foot, wrenched it off and threw it into a corner of the room. Wrapping his hands around the wound, he drew new skin over it and banished the pain. Then he vanished. Matheus slept peacefully and woke next morning to find the stump healed. His mother returned to find him recovered, able to walk happily with the aid of a stick, a lump of rotting flesh festering in the corner of the room.

The masons take up their work with particular vigour, fearing the power of the Holy Cross should they be seen to be slacking.

John of Battle proves his ability to serve his king well and after completing the Stamford cross goes on to build those at Stony Stratford, Dunstable, St Albans and Hardingstone.

*

To the disappointment of the masons when they arrive at Dunstable Priory in the spring of 1292 they find the welcome they receive from the canons to be less hospitable than they hoped. The canons are, it seems, mindful of a royal visit in 1275 that few can now remember but has been much spoken about among their community ever since. On that occasion the king's falconers abused the hospitality of the priory and from that time the canons have held the king's servants in suspicion. The falconers behaved disgracefully, turning on the servants of the priory, demanding more drink even though they had already had more than enough. In the resulting mayhem the chaplain was killed. At the time the canons were dismayed that the king was inclined to believe the claim of his falconers, that the servants of the priory did not show them due respect. The view of the canons was later vindicated by the verdict of a jury of thirty-six men that it was the falconers who were in the wrong.

John of Battle goes to great lengths to assure the canons that there will be no lack of respect and instructs the masons to show their humility by praying at the famous shrine of St Fremund in the priory church. Fremund was a devout hermit in the early years of Christianity who heard a calling from God to lead the Saxons against Danish invasion. He won a decisive victory but was killed by one of his own men, jealous of his success. After his death miracles occurred at his burial place. Some of his bones were later brought to the priory at Dunstable, where their mysterious potency attracts many pilgrims.

Once the cross is complete, it can be seen from miles around. It is placed on a mound so that it can be seen clearly from the great highway of Watling Street that passes through the town. This important route is the link between the ports of Kent and far off Holyhead from where the ships to Ireland depart. Just five years previously the king found the prior of the abbey to be negligent in repairing this crucial road and ordered him to repair the ruts.

Later that autumn people of all kinds, knights and their ladies, servants and tradesmen, will descend in their hundreds for the tournament that has been planned. The Eleanor Cross will be their beacon as they approach the town, inviting a prayer for her on their safe arrival.

*

Proud of all the commissions he has been given, John of Battle is glad of the one in St Albans, his home town. His family also are pleased that he can remain with them and not be undertaking a long and dangerous journey. After many years of work at King Edward's Abbey, Vale Royal, in Cheshire, Master John settled in the town of St Albans. There he worked on the abbey where building had long been progressing to create a structure fit to house the shrine of the first English martyr, St Alban.

The tomb of St Alban was rediscovered in 1257, during the reign of King Edward's father, King Henry, when the town was struck by a severe earthquake causing irreparable damage to the apse at the eastern end of the abbey. It was demolished to reveal ancient bricks from Roman Imperial times and a paving slab, which was lifted to reveal the original burial place of St Alban. The monks fell to their knees in wonder. They saw now that the earthquake, which had seemed to be a terrible calamity, was God's way of directing them towards this holy spot.

Lying on top of Alban's coffin was a cross with a large circular head that made it look uncannily like the form of a man, arms stretched out. This was said to be the first cross brought to England which Alban held in his hands as he was executed. Alongside his shrine were discovered bones of the twelve apostles of Christ, brought from Rome by a bishop of the abbey many centuries before.

The bishop decreed that the occasion should be marked by the construction of a marvellous shrine for the saint and the abbey should be rebuilt in his honour. He envisaged a great building with spacious processional routes for the many pilgrims who would be drawn here.

That work still continues and pilgrims are indeed moved to come to the abbey in ever greater numbers, the poor and sick, praying for saintly intervention to help them with their struggles. Many leave rewarded for their faith, wounds healed, sight restored, children brought back from the dead. All those visitors will now also be inspired to offer a prayer for Queen Eleanor as they pass by her cross that dominates the market square.

*

Edward sets great store by the physical reminders he has created for Eleanor but he knows full well that the laying down of memories in the minds of his subjects takes more than stone and mortar. He does not intend to leave the offering of prayers to the whim of the people but goes to great lengths to ensure the regular taking of Mass in Eleanor's honour, making many endowments for their observation.

The most significant provision he makes is to Westminster Abbey in 1292, to which he gives twenty-two manors from Eleanor's estate to fund the celebration of Mass in her memory. He specifies in great detail how the ceremonies are to be observed. On Monday of each week the entire abbey is to gather for the singing of hymns, reading of lessons and tolling of bells. Silver pennies are to be distributed to as many as 140 paupers who are each then required to recite prayers for Eleanor's soul. While the giving of alms in Eleanor's name will encourage God to look favourably upon her soul, the prayers of thanks that follow will further serve to protect it from the pains of Purgatory.

Each anniversary of Eleanor's death is to be as elaborate as the funeral itself, with every noble in England expected to attend. On that occasion services are to continue from six o'clock in the evening through the night until after high Mass the next morning, while the bells of the monastery ring unceasingly. Provision is made for a hundred candles to burn around her tomb. Alms are to be given to the poor, the mendicant friars and the London hospitals. Similar chantries for the regular observation of Mass are also founded at Blackfriars Priory and at smaller churches across the realm. Edward authorises many other endowments throughout the country. In one particular transaction he agrees to a transfer of land to Peterborough Abbey on condition that two of its chaplains celebrate Mass for Eleanor on a daily basis with three services on the anniversary of her death.

Numerous benefactors follow Edward's lead in ensuring that prayers will always be offered for Eleanor's soul. In April 1291 the Archbishop of York orders prayers to be said for her in all the churches under his control, with forty days remission from Purgatory for those who oblige. The following June he is able to inform Edward that no fewer than 47,528 Masses have been celebrated for the queen within the diocese.

In 1294 a chantry chapel at the Church of All Saints in Harby, Eleanor's place of death, dedicated to the celebration of Masses in perpetuity for her soul, funded by the Archbishop of York, is ready for consecration. By this time, four years since the loss of Eleanor, a great deal has taken place in the realm, war erupting with both Scotland and France. Edward now looks back on those last years with Eleanor as a golden time, his kingdom at peace, his queen by his side. He has never ceased to think of her, in spite of all the demands on his attention and leadership. Perhaps, he wonders, if Eleanor were with him still, she, with her perceptive intelligence, would have alerted him sooner to the duplicity of the French and war on two fronts could have been avoided. Additionally, recent rebellion in Wales where his prized castle at Caernarvon has been seized and others placed under siege, demand renewed military action, his greatest immediate concern.

However pressing the call to Wales Edward is insistent on first returning to Harby for the service of consecration, conducted by the Archbishop of York. He is to be assisted by Roger de Newton, selected as the first holder of the office of Chantry Priest for Queen Eleanor. Given the significance of the role, he and future incumbents are to be rewarded with a generous income for carrying out their duties, performing the daily Mass for Eleanor, with additional prayers offered on anniversaries of her birth, marriage and death. Edward is anxious to meet Roger de Newton personally, to impress upon this young priest the gravity of his duties. He feels he must make certain of the intensity of the young priest's devotion, knowing that its strength will increase the potency of his delivery of Mass.

The service of dedication is attended by Richard de Weston, in whose home Eleanor died. His properties have now been enhanced through the king's payments in gratitude for his hospitality when the queen was so gravely ill. He again makes his home available for the royal entourage, although he still feels unworthy of addressing the king directly. As he attends the service Edward adds his prayers to the many that have already been offered, in the hope that she has by now been spared yet more suffering.

Following the consecration of the chantry chapel at Harby, Edward, against the advice of his lords, still resists the call to Wales. Instead he travels to Lincoln for the service of consecration of Eleanor's viscera tomb in the Angel Choir of the cathedral, led by Bishop Sutton. Returning to the Angel Choir has particular poignancy for Edward, this being the place that Eleanor never reached when struck down by illness.

The marble tomb chest is the work of Alexander of Abingdon and Dymenge de Reyns, heraldic shields around its sides. Fixed upon it is the remarkable bronze effigy made by William Torel. Its arrival at Lincoln from Westminster was a considerable achievement, the great weight of the bronze requiring the efforts of several men to cart it up the hill to the cathedral and to lift it into place.

Edward remembers vividly the occasion of the consecration of the choir and translation of the relics of St Hugh in 1284, sixty-five years after the canonisation of the saint, when he and Eleanor were here together. The pope had been sufficiently concerned about the delay that he decreed a forty-day remission from Purgatory for all those contributing to the fabric fund for the building of the choir or who attended the occasion of the translation of the relics. With Edward and Eleanor among the contributors, at long last the money was raised to complete the choir in a way worthy of the saint. It was some comfort to Edward that the pope's decree was to be of direct benefit to Eleanor.

Now, with many gathered for the consecration of Eleanor's tomb, the choir is, as then, bathed in the morning light that streams in through the vast eight-light east window, nearly sixty feet tall, throwing into relief the fine carvings, as if God were giving clarity to the world. The immaculate polish of the Purbeck marble shafts that support the vaulted roof shines like dancing lights. Edward's eye follows the columns upwards to the intricate patterns of the stone ribs above his head. On the bosses at the meeting points he can pick out perfect replications of a whole array of different kinds of leaves.

In the triangular areas of the wall surfaces between the curves of the arches are carvings of angels, thirty of them, all showing different scenes. Directly above the shrine of St Hugh the angels associated with the Last Judgement give way to a choir of angels, wings extended and playing musical instruments. Their music-making serves to remind the faithful of the celestial bliss that is the privilege of the saint in Heaven.

The angel on which Edward's gaze finally settles is a depiction of the archangel Michael who holds the scales for the weighing of the souls of the departed. Edward's thoughts dwell on the wellbeing of Eleanor as she is judged by this measure. He prays that his commemoration of her has been enough for the balance to tip in her favour.

*

By the autumn of 1294 the tomb for Eleanor in Westminster Abbey, even more elaborate than that in Lincoln Cathedral, is ready for consecration, occupying its honoured position in the chapel of Edward the Confessor. It was a piece of good fortune that the master mason, Richard of Crundale, was able to complete the tomb chest itself, carved from solid Purbeck marble of the highest quality, before his untimely death. Its faces are decorated with shields hung on delicate tree branches bearing the arms of England, Castile, León and Ponthieu. Inscribed in beautiful lettering around its lid are the words written in the French language that Edward and Eleanor conversed in:

Here lies Eleanor, sometime Queen of England, wife of King Edward son of King Henry, and daughter of the King of Spain and Countess of Ponthieu, on whose soul God in His pity have mercy. Amen.

Edward cannot be more impassioned in the appeal for God's mercy. The beautiful bronze effigy that it supports is acknowledged by all to be a masterpiece. Her head rests as if in sleep on two overlapping cushions, covered with the repeated pattern of the castle for Castile. Although of unforgiving metal, her pillows seem to give comfort as they support Eleanor's head. Her crown and the fringes of her garments are inlaid with jewels. The flat metal plate on which she lies is patterned with the castle and the leopard of England. Enclosing the whole structure is an ornate wooden canopy, vaulted and with intricate carved bosses that glitter with gilt crafted by the master carpenter, Thomas de Hokyntone. It is a vision of Heaven ready to welcome Eleanor on judgement day.

The canopy and the plinth of the chest are painted by Master Walter of Durham. The side of the plinth is adorned with a depiction of the king and queen's loyal adviser, Sir Otto de Grandson. Both were deeply grateful for the support over many years of Sir Otto, who accompanied them on many of their journeys abroad. Of all their loyal advisers it is his image that King Edward chose to decorate the tomb of Queen Eleanor. Sir Otto is depicted, together with four pilgrims, kneeling in prayer before the Virgin and Child at the Holy Sepulchre in Jerusalem. His devout stance will, Edward is confident, encourage the prayers of visitors to the tomb for Eleanor.

The whole structure is surrounded by an iron grille by the master smith, Thomas of Leighton. There were concerns about the awarding of the commission for the metalwork as the king's previous master smith, Henry of Lewes, died suddenly in 1291. Master Thomas was summoned at short notice having been commended by Bishop Sutton who had seen a beautiful iron screen made by him when consecrating a church at Leighton Buzzard. Master Thomas' work for the abbey is of great elegance, with foliate scrolls riveted to vertical iron bars and delicate stamped rosettes fixed to the end of the frame. The tops of the bars end in prongs on which candles are fixed, the whole structure bowing outwards so the flames clear the wooden canopy above.

The lords of the realm gather to show their respect at the consecration service, as they did at the funeral. None can fail to experience a sense of awe as the patina of the bronze effigy glints in the candle light, the atmosphere heady with incense. As the king kneels on the beautiful pavement in front of the altar, he is deeply aware of Eleanor's absence, nothing but slabs of bare cold stone in the place where she was beside him on so many occasions. He hopes that at least his prayers can reach her.

The sumptuous tomb that Edward commissioned to hold the hearts of Eleanor and their son, Alphonso, is now complete and it is now time for the service of consecration.

It is surrounded by statues of the queen and Virgin Mary in canopied niches looking down upon it. They are carved by the hand of Alexander of Abingdon himself, the flowing lines of the drapery displaying his artistry. As the king looks up into the faces of the statues it is possible to imagine the figures stepping out from their fixings under the elaborate canopies, their robes swaying with the movement of their bodies as they walk towards him. With so many images of Eleanor looking down at him, the king senses her one day reaching out to him from Heaven, smiling.

Valuable gold and jewels are set into the surface of the tomb chest, giving it the appearance of a delicate casket for precious relics, the work of Adam the Goldsmith. The whole tomb sparkles as the rays of the sun are deflected onto it through the painted glass in the windows, shedding coloured light into the chapel. The carving on the tomb is aglow with colour, every detail of the worked stone freshly picked out in paint, deep reds, blues and greens. Standing above the tomb, watching over it, is the figure of an angel holding a golden heart, also made by Adam the Goldsmith. All the free wall surfaces are filled with intricate pictures, depictions of the life of the virgin, by the hand of the master, Walter of Durham.

Edward trusts that Eleanor and their son will soon be reunited in Heaven as their hearts are on earth and he will join them when his time comes. He leaves in the knowledge that these remains are safe in the hands of the Blackfriars, assured of their true devotion.

5.

EDWARD AFTER ELEANOR

Within four years of the death of Queen Eleanor all twelve memorial crosses and three tombs are finished, a significant achievement. The royal masons have served the king well in completing their tasks smoothly, ensuring that materials were ordered and delivered on time, workers paid and standards of workmanship maintained. Edward can now feel confident in the prayers of the people for Eleanor.

During the latter part of his reign Edward continues to support the work of his favoured masons. After the completion of the Cheapside Cross, Michael of Canterbury is, in 1292, given the commission for the construction of the tomb of King Edward's brother, Edmund Crouchback, Earl of Lancaster, in Westminster Abbey. He goes on to build the tomb of Archbishop Pecham in 1296 at Canterbury Cathedral. He is also given the highly prestigious task of building the new St Stephen's Chapel in the Palace of Westminster. Here he is given the opportunity to elaborate on the four-centred arch form, which sweeps to the point at its apex in a curve that turns back on itself. First tentatively used on the Eleanor Crosses, this shape is now used to create a whole building of great elegance and delicacy. Edward is forced reluctantly to bring his plans for the construction of this prestigious building to a halt in 1307 due to the pressing financial demands of a new war with Scotland.

Alexander of Abingdon receives many more notable commissions for figurative sculpture, much of it to adorn the tombs built by Michael of Canterbury. The painter, Master Walter, is kept busy with further work at the royal Palace of Westminster and at the palace of the Archbishop of York.

THE ELEANOR CROSSES

William Torel continues to work as royal goldsmith until 1303 when scandal strikes Westminster Abbey with the audacious robbery of the king's treasury in the crypt below the Chapter House. Many of the monks come under suspicion of having carefully planned the robbery over many months and are imprisoned in the Tower of London.

Among the treasures taken is the jewelled case, in the shape of a Celtic cross, for the Cross of Neith. This cross is nothing less than a fragment of the True Cross on which Christ was crucified and was in the possession of the Welsh princes until seized by King Edward as a trophy of his conquest of Wales. Its significance to Edward is shown by the considerable sums of money that he spent on having the case encrusted with gem stones.

Although not involved in the thefts, William Torel is found to have purchased plate that came from the king's treasury, thereby irrevocably damaging his reputation. He dies soon after, denied the opportunity to return to royal favour.

After Eleanor's death Edward adds to his collection of trophies of the Welsh princes that he holds in Westminster Abbey with the acquisition of Scottish royal regalia. His greatest prize is the Stone of Scone, used in the coronation of every King of Scotland for many centuries, taken from Scone Abbey when on a victory tour in 1306. This precious symbol of Scottish sovereignty is placed on the steps by the shrine of The Confessor. Adam, the royal goldsmith, has been commissioned to create an elaborate bronze chair to house the stone, as befits its importance. Unfortunately the costs of the king's wars mean that this could not be afforded and a simple wooden chair has been made instead. In 1307 the king decides that the chair must at least be enhanced and the painter Walter of Durham is commissioned to decorate it with patterns of birds, foliage and animals on a gilt ground, the figure of King Edward on the back.

With the memorials to Eleanor achieved, Edward is being encouraged by his advisers to remarry. Indeed, with just one surviving son, Edward of Caernarvon, there is pressure on him to do so. Nonetheless, it is not until September 1299, nearly nine years after Eleanor's death, that he finally does so. At the age of nearly sixty, as part of a negotiated peace treaty, he marries Margaret, the twenty-year-old sister of King Philip IV of France, in Canterbury Cathedral. It is agreed also that Prince Edward will marry King Philip's daughter, Isabella.

Edward grows fond of his young wife, who is known for her beauty, named 'The Flower of France' by the chroniclers. Even so, his loyalty to Eleanor endures and Margaret is never crowned. Shortly after their marriage, while Edward is occupied with organising the fight against Scotland, Margaret spends three weeks at St Albans Abbey. There she sees the Eleanor Cross where she prays for the blessing of her predecessor. Her prayers are answered and she bears King Edward two healthy sons, born in 1300 and 1301, Thomas and Edmund. A baby girl, born in 1306, is named Eleanor in memory of the queen.

*

In the summer of 1307 King Edward is in inhospitable terrain in the far north of England, leading his troops in the war against Scotland. Refusing to give in to lingering and painful illness, he is determined to achieve victory and understands what a vital part his leadership plays in the battle. He musters his soldiers at Carlisle and, refusing to be borne on the litter that has carried him this far, insists upon being seen riding his war-horse. Such is the gravity of his condition that after ten days he has advanced only six miles.

In spite of his conviction that he must win the war against Scotland before he dies, he can no longer fight off the ravages of disease. His health deteriorates further and on 7 July, at the age of sixty-eight, he dies in the arms of his attendants as they support him to eat. At the time of his death he is the oldest king who has ever reigned over England.

For almost two weeks his demise is kept a closely guarded secret, his advisers fearing that the devastating news will galvanise the morale of the Scottish armies. Only Queen Margaret, John Dalderby, the Bishop of Lincoln, and his son by Eleanor, Prince Edward of Caernarvon, are informed. Those who dare to speak of it risk imprisonment. Edward, his twenty-three-year-old heir, receives the news on 11 July and immediately sets off north. As must inevitably happen, he is acknowledged as King Edward II at Carlisle Castle on 20 July and the veil of secrecy is lifted at last.

The deceased king's body begins its long journey south, led by Walter Langton, Bishop of Coventry. The new King Edward is able to accompany his father's funeral cortège for only part of the way as he is obliged to return north to lead the Scottish campaign. It is not until 4 August, two weeks later, that the procession is received by the monks of Waltham Abbey, as progress is slowed by the throngs of lamenting subjects trying to touch the coffin.

The king's body lies in the abbey church in the same spot where that of Eleanor rested. It remains there for more than two months, until 18 October, when the new King Edward is finally able to return from battle in Scotland. Only then is it taken from Waltham Abbey for the journey to London, resting over successive nights in several of the churches of the city.

In St Paul's Cathedral Londoners pour through, jostling to pay their respects at the coffin of their greatly revered king. It is laid alongside the shrine containing the bones of St Erkenwald, patron saint of the City of London and one of the first bishops of this magnificent cathedral at the time when England had yet to become a fully Christian kingdom. It is the aura that surrounds his relics that has established the importance of this place, a place worthy of being a resting place for the deceased monarch.

Erkenwald's fame began with his work as a missionary and he was renowned for converting many of the Saxon rulers and their families to Christianity. During his travels evidence of his sanctity was noticed. His most astonishing miracle occurred when he was presiding over the building of the cathedral, as a tomb containing a perfectly preserved body was revealed. Its interior was painted with gold, the corpse dressed in golden robes decorated with pearls and fur-trimmed cloak, all as bright as the day they were made. The dead man opened his eyes and spoke, explaining that he was a pagan leader from centuries before the birth of Christ. His body had remained intact in anticipation of the Christian baptism that would allow him to find eternal bliss in Heaven. Meanwhile his restless soul remained languishing in Limbo. Erkenwald duly baptised the pagan with his tears and the body instantly turned to dust, the soul of the deceased at last freed to find peace in Heaven.

After Erkenwald's death his relics were preserved in his cathedral. Their miraculous powers held strong, their aura giving protection to the body of King Edward as they had to Eleanor's seventeen years before.

*

On 27 October the funeral of the king is at last held at Westminster Abbey, nearly four months after his death. He is to be buried here, next to his father and his beloved Eleanor, even though there are rumours that on his deathbed he requested his heart to be sent to the Holy Land and his bones to be carried at the head of the army in Scotland until it is conquered.

The praise for Edward I is boundless. This illustrious king is spoken of as the noblest ruler since Arthur, even since Alexander the Great, ruler of the ancient Macedonian empire. The deceased King Edward takes his place in the Chapel of The Confessor, his body dressed in full coronation garb, bearing a crown and sceptre. This is not the death of a mere mortal but of an anointed monarch, his God-given powers now passing to his son.

Surrounded on all sides by tombs of elaborate splendour, that of Edward I is of remarkable simplicity, a massive box of black marble, five thick slabs, over nine and a half feet in length and three and a half feet high. It is completely plain but for the shaping of the corners of the lid, inviting the suggestion that such a great king warrants greater splendours in death.

But the choice of a tomb of such starkness is not a mark of disrespect by his son. Rather it is an expression of a personal choice by the late king. Edward, aware of the power of symbolism until the end of his life, planned his sepulchre to be a replica of the tomb of the legendary British ruler, King Arthur. It was into a tomb at Glastonbury Abbey of similar simple grandeur which he and Eleanor together watched the remains of Arthur and his queen, Guinevere, being reinterred in 1278.

Although King Edward has died without achieving his vision of uniting the island of Britain he is thus making clear his ambition to do so. By imitating Arthur's tomb, even in death Edward makes a symbolic statement of his authority and ambition to rule over the whole of the island of Britain: England, Wales and now Scotland. The simplicity of the tomb speaks of the simplicity of his message, that here lies a worthy successor to Arthur's crown with his Guinevere, Eleanor, beside him.

Part II

THE LIVES OF THE CROSSES

Eleanor of Castile is now little remembered. It is often thought that she gave her name to The Elephant and Castle in London, a corruption of La Infanta Castilla, The Princess of Castile. Spanish princesses were not, however, known as *infantas* until the seventeenth century. Nor was Charing a derivation of a term of affection allegedly used by Edward for Eleanor, *chère reine*. The village of Charing existed long before the time of Edward and Eleanor.

The name of Eleanor of Castile survives in the Eleanor Crosses. Edward's creation stood in the landscape for over two hundred years, time and decay taking their natural toll. But during the sixteenth century, everything would change. As a result of major political and religious upheavals Eleanor's legacy was to be profoundly affected in both material and symbolic ways.

Although most of the crosses themselves did survive that period of turbulence, their days were nonetheless numbered. A second phase of violent disruption in the seventeenth century had a catastrophic and irreversible impact on the enduring physical reminders of Eleanor.

Yet there were some survivals into the eighteenth century and beyond. In spite of concerted attempts to destroy the past, the ripple effect of Eleanor's legacy did live on through the agency of art and ideas. The next section takes up the story of the crosses themselves through these periods of destruction and then reclamation.

An eighteenth-century engraving of the Waltham Cross (Library of Congress, Washington DC).

6.

ELEANOR IN THE REFORMATION

In 1501, more than two hundred years after the death of Eleanor of Castile, another Spanish princess arrived in England. Katherine of Aragon was, like Eleanor, a young bride destined to be queen. Both princesses shared ancestry in the royal house of Castile, both marriages were dynastic arrangements. The fifteen-year-old Katherine was to be married to Arthur, son and heir to the founding monarch of the Tudor dynasty, Henry VII.

Katherine was the daughter of two of the most powerful rulers in Europe, the Queen of Castile and the King of Aragon. Her royal blood line was highly prestigious. Like Arthur, she could trace her roots back to John of Gaunt through both his first and second marriages, a stronger link than her young husband could claim. This union would therefore serve to further augment and establish the Tudor dynasty.

Like Eleanor, Katherine came from Mediterranean climes to an English October. Her sea voyage up the Atlantic coast of France had been treacherous. The first attempt to sail was disrupted by storms so severe that the ship's masts were ripped from their sockets and she was forced to turn back. When she did at last reach London her arrival was, as Eleanor's had been, the occasion of joyful celebration, the streets decorated in her honour. After a night at Lambeth Palace, the seat of the Archbishop of Canterbury, Katherine processed through the city of London, her passage marked by a series of elaborate pageants. Turning from Gracechurch Street into Cornhill, she reached Cheapside, where she passed the Eleanor Cross to reach St Paul's Cathedral for the marriage ceremony. It was here that she was to meet Prince Arthur for the first time.

At fifteen years old, her betrothed was the same age that Edward I had been at the time of his marriage. She would have hoped deeply that her marriage to Arthur would be as auspicious as Edward's was to Eleanor. Sadly this was not to be. In fact, as a direct result of it, the world in which Eleanor and Edward lived, worked and prayed was to be altered beyond all recognition. And the great memorial legacy of Edward to his wife, left virtually untouched for more than two centuries, was about to be called into question as never before.

The prince to whom Katherine was betrothed had been named Arthur in unambiguous reference to the legendary British King Arthur. Just as Caernarvon was picked as the birthplace of the future Edward II for symbolic reasons, the birth of this Tudor Prince of Wales was arranged to take place at Winchester Castle. This auspicious place was considered to be the site of King Arthur's court of Camelot, the Great Hall still containing the round table where he and his knights had sat. Henry Tudor was making an unambiguous inference that his new dynasty was worthy of Arthur's crown, the fascination with Arthurian legend holding as strong as it did at the time of Edward I. Henry Tudor invoked the words of Merlin who had described the infant King Arthur as the fruit of the union between the red king and white queen. In doing so he was making a comparison with his own son, the product of the royal houses of Lancaster and York, symbolised by the red and white roses.

Henry VII's Lancastrian claim to regal ancestry was tenuous and he was anxious to find ways to reinforce it. His royal heritage was through his mother's line, she being a direct descendant of the Plantagenet kings through John of Gaunt, a great-grandson of King Edward I and Eleanor. But the link was weakened since this line of descent came through the offspring of John of Gaunt's third wife, who gave birth to his children before wedlock. Having won the crown by deposing the Yorkist King Richard III, Henry Tudor tried to strengthen his position through marriage to Elizabeth of York, Richard's niece. Her own status as a royal princess was coloured by bloodshed and intrigue, her brothers being the tragic Princes in the Tower, allegedly murdered by Richard III. The boys were last seen alive in their uncle's care on their way to London in one of the many inns that had grown up in Stony Stratford since Queen Eleanor's cortège stopped there more than 200 years previously.

Henry Tudor's plans for the future of the monarchy were thrown into disarray when Prince Arthur, aged fifteen, died only five months after the marriage. Katherine remained in England and seven years later, in 1509, was married to his younger brother, who had recently been crowned as King Henry VIII.

The childhood of Henry VIII had been lived against the background of the precariousness of the new Tudor dynasty with numerous challenges to the throne. Acutely aware that the Tudors were newcomers to the royal families of Christendom, Henry VIII was driven by a passion to produce a son and heir, and was eager to emphasise his link to the kings of the island of Britain through his father's Welsh heritage. Learned works such as *Anglia Historia* of 1534 by Polydore Vergil, Archdeacon of Wells, argued that the Tudors were in direct line of descent from the heroic King Arthur who was in turn descended from the Emperor Constantine and his British mother, St Helena. Where Edward I had asserted his authority over Arthur by burying him and appropriating Welsh legend for his own ends, Henry was going one better and claiming a link through blood.

Henry's Arthurian enthusiasms were such that when he entertained the visiting Holy Roman Emperor, Charles V, at Winchester Castle in 1522, the feast was held in the Great Hall, its round table the focal point. He had it repainted for the occasion, picturing King Arthur in state with sword and orb, his face in Henry's own image. At the centre was the Tudor rose, the rim divided into twenty-four segments, each named for one of Arthur's knights.

The union of King Henry and Queen Katherine was soon blessed with a son—Henry, Duke of Cornwall who was born in 1511. The king and queen, both profound believers in the power of relics, walked to the shrine of The Virgin at Walsingham Abbey to pray for his wellbeing. In a tradition upheld since the time of Edward I, they showed their penitence by leaving their shoes in the Slipper Chapel, a mile and a half from the shrine, and walked the rest of the way barefooted. It was a striking sight to see the strong and athletic King Henry, like Edward I six feet two inches tall in his stockinged feet, showing such humility. It was Katherine's tragedy that their prayers were unanswered and the baby died just a few weeks later.

In spite of this heartbreak, they continued to have hope, King Henry holding his wife in high esteem. In 1513 Henry was abroad in France pursuing military glory by winning back territories that had previously been under English rule. Henry chose Katherine to be Governor of the Realm and Captain General of the King's Forces in his absence, a position of weighty responsibility. In this capacity she found herself called upon to organise resistance to a Scottish invasion. She was widely commended for delivering a rousing speech to the troops, dressed in full armour, even though she was once again in an advanced state of pregnancy. Later, at Woburn Abbey she was given as a trophy the bloodied coat of the slain King James IV of Scotland after his invasion was repelled at Flodden in Northumberland.

The Eleanor Cross, still standing at the gates of Woburn Abbey after more than two hundred years, was there as the focal point for the queen's prayers of thanks and hopes that the child she was carrying would be a healthy boy. She could not have known that it would be the slain king of Scots and not her husband who would be a future great-grandfather to a King of England.

For all her devotion to God, Queen Katherine was even unluckier with her pregnancies than Queen Eleanor had been. Henry's delight at the Flodden victory was shattered when she gave birth to a stillborn son just a month later. That tragedy was followed the next year by the death of another boy who survived only a few weeks. Katherine finally gave birth to a healthy child in 1516, but in those times when only male monarchs were generally considered capable of ruling, little Princess Mary was not the answer to her parents' prayers.

Still loyal to his wife, King Henry enlarged the royal apartments at Leeds Castle in Kent, where she took up residence in 1519. In this favoured residence of King Edward and Queen Eleanor, Katherine's suite of rooms overlooked the artificial lake created by Edward—the very view that Queen Eleanor would have enjoyed more than two hundred years previously. It was in the chantry chapel that Edward I built within the castle walls and endowed for Eleanor that Queen Katherine said her prayers.

But by 1533 Queen Katherine was over forty years old with no hope of further pregnancies, and with only one daughter surviving from her six pregnancies. The king's commitment to his wife was now exhausted and he was determined to seek an annulment of his marriage in order to remarry and, he hoped, secure a legitimate male heir. By so doing he was in defiance of the papacy which had declared the marriage valid.

King Henry's opposition to the authority of the pope, the leader of the Church and God's representative on earth, was a challenge that was to have then unimaginable ramifications. Henry met his advisers, the Archbishop of Canterbury, Thomas Cranmer, and the Bishops of Hereford and Winchester, in Waltham Abbey to discuss the possibility of divorce. This religious house had for centuries been connected with royalty. It was much favoured by King Harold, the last King of England before the Norman Conquest. Harold lost his life at the Battle of Hastings in 1066, defending his throne from the invasion led by William, Duke of Normandy. His mutilated body was identified by his wife, Edith Swan-Neck, who was permitted by the victorious Duke William to take his body for burial at Waltham.

Henry VIII owned a property by the abbey gates, in the area of the town known as Romeland. He frequently visited to enjoy the hunting as well as observing religious devotions, praying to the Holy Cross before which the coffins of Eleanor and Edward had lain centuries before.

The divorce proceedings finally opened in the Lady Chapel of the church of Dunstable Priory, attended by Archbishop Cranmer and the most important bishops in England. Queen Katherine was cited to appear but she chose not to attend, refusing to accept that this court had jurisdiction over the decision of the pope. On 23 May 1533 Archbishop Cranmer found the marriage to be null and void and the notice of its annulment was fixed to the church door. A short distance away, still standing at the crossroads, was the Eleanor Cross, a memorial to such a different royal marriage.

*

The king, having freed himself of Katherine, now made plans for the coronation of Anne Boleyn. The ceremony was to take place in June 1533 and celebrated with great extravagance. The Cheapside Eleanor Cross, symbolising the continuity of monarchy, was re-gilded for the occasion. The following year the Act of Supremacy was passed by which the king was declared head of the Church in England and no longer accountable to the pope.

Henry's break with the Roman Catholic Church, putting England on the path towards becoming a Protestant country, was to have radical implications for people's understanding of their relationship with God and expression of faith. Although there had been murmurings of dissent from the Catholic faith in England throughout the previous century and before, such thinking had been regarded as heresy. Henry himself was still entirely immersed in traditional Catholic expressions of belief. With his divorce and excommunication from the Church of Rome, the Protestant view that its doctrines obscured the direct relationship between God and the individual was to gain sway. The worship of saints, the cult of relics and belief in Purgatory, previously fundamental to an understanding of mankind's place in the universe, were all called into question and a new, simplified form of religious expression was imposed.

According to the Protestant faith, the relationship of the devout was directly with God, a private and personal connection. The purpose of Mass under Protestantism was no longer to establish a transaction with those in Heaven but to strengthen the faith of the individual, with the place for the intercession of saints significantly reduced. The concept of Purgatory was now precluded, there no longer being a need for a transitional place between Heaven and Hell. Indeed, Purgatory was now denounced as a cynical means by which the priesthood could exploit superstitious gullibility and fear of death for its own financial advantage.

With England at the beginning of a process of change that was to lead to Protestantism, in 1535 King Henry turned his attention to the monasteries. The king was under enormous financial pressure and was enticed by their riches. The monastic system had existed since the dawn of Christianity and over the centuries monasteries had become wealthy and powerful. Many performed important social functions such as teaching and caring for the sick. But their accumulated riches offered a great enticement for King Henry, as ever needing money to fill his war chest.

Looking for reasons to close them, the king sent his commissioners to inspect the abbeys, in search of evidence of monastic corruption and the promotion of superstition, relics and stories of feigned miracles. They found numerous examples of endowments made to support Masses for the dead, like those for Eleanor, being misappropriated and charitable donations stolen. There was evidence in abundance of degeneracy, such as drinking after compline, rendering the monks incapable of rising to perform the night services. Tales were rife of pig bones being passed off as relics of saints and of monks stage-managing miracles to dupe gullible pilgrims.

The commissioners compiled detailed inventories of the vast numbers of relics held in monasteries across the country. These were then stripped of precious jewels and metals, rich pickings for King Henry. At Westminster Abbey the intricate inlaid gem stones were roughly prised out of the shrine of Edward the Confessor, leaving a damaged pedestal. The monks took the precaution of hiding the wooden coffin containing the body itself. His precious ring with which he was buried and which had been removed from his finger for preservation with the abbey's treasures after his canonisation in 1163 also disappeared.

The shrine containing the head of St Hugh in Lincoln Cathedral that Queen Eleanor had been striving to reach during the final stages of her illness disappeared without trace. The Holy Cross from Waltham Abbey and the phial of Christ's blood from Ashridge Priory were also casualties.

Sacred objects of little material value, which had been revered and carefully preserved through the centuries, were destroyed. A number of these items may have been cynically manufactured by the monks but there were those that had been considered sacred for generations. Artefacts that had been part of people's lives, from kings to commoners, were held up for ridicule and denied them. At Westminster Abbey hundreds of such treasures were lost, including Our Lady's girdle, an object which had given comfort to generations of queens during childbirth, among them Queen Eleanor herself. Other items named on the abbey inventory included a part of the manger, some of the frankincense offered by the Magi, a piece of the table of the last supper together with some of the bread, part of the cross on which Christ was crucified, fragments of the sponge, spear and scourge, some of the Virgin's milk, a lock of her hair, part of her bed, and a piece of the window by which the angel stood at the Annunciation.

The commissioners' report was presented to Parliament in 1536. Monastic houses with revenues of under £200 were dissolved immediately while the richer ones were given a respite of two or three years. A set of Articles was issued restricting the traditional reliance on saints and intercession on behalf of souls in Purgatory. An Act of Parliament followed abolishing all feast days to commemorate saints apart from those in celebration of the Apostles, the Blessed Virgin, John the Baptist and St George and some notable days such as All Saints Day, Ascension Day and Candlemas. The long-established pattern of ritual observance that had defined the calendar year, with its multitude of local festivals and major dates, was overturned. The recognition given to such previously significant saints as Edward the Confessor, Alban and Hugh of Lincoln ceased. Pilgrimages were also now forbidden, a development which was to have a pronounced impact on the livelihoods of towns such as St Albans.

*

In 1538 it was the turn of St Katherine's Priory in Lincoln to be dissolved. The jewelled reliquaries, gold and silver plate and rich furnishings had already gone. The last prior, William Griffiths, was now forced to surrender the buildings and its lands to the crown. Since the building of the Eleanor Cross, previously at the gates to the city, the priory grounds had expanded to encompass it.

Lead from the roofs and gutters was unceremoniously thrown into carts to be sold for the benefit of the king. Other items were auctioned. Much of what could not be easily removed was cursorily smashed, the Eleanor Cross badly damaged in the process.

Prior Griffiths and the thirteen remaining canons were given pensions and sent to find their own way while the lay sisters received nothing. The king gave the land to his brother-in-law, Charles Brandon, Duke of Suffolk, who made no use of it. For the next two years the priory stood empty and neglected. The once beautiful buildings rapidly deteriorated, with little protection from stormy weather, left to the mercies of encroaching wildlife and vagrants in search of shelter.

THE ELEANOR CROSSES

The Duke of Suffolk sold the estate to a Vincent Grantham, a local man whose family had become rich over several previous generations through the wool trade. Grantham, Member of Parliament for the area, surveyed his new property with pride. While in the time of Edward and Eleanor only royalty and a handful of aristocrats could live in any degree of comfort, such an aspiration was now within the grasp of a man such as Grantham, a man who believed himself to be deserving of the material rewards that this world could offer. He wanted a home he could be proud of, a family seat to be passed to his son in turn. The draughty, now decaying priory buildings were swept aside to make way for a modern building with fire places in all the rooms, separate areas for family and servants and wide, generous windows. The grounds, previously given over to growing vegetables, were replanted in the fashionable style, with intricate beds of flowers and herbs.

There was no place here for the damaged Eleanor Cross. This crumbling memorial to a forgotten queen from times long past was now worth little more than its weight as rubble. It was with no regret that he ordered the stones to be knocked down and broken up and thrown into the foundations of his new house.

Grantham saved just one of the statues, not out of superstition or reverence, but because he rather liked the graciously smiling face and swirling robes, as if the queen were about to step forward to dance. He thought he would keep it as a memento to decorate the kitchen garden.

The fate met by Woburn Abbey, also in 1538, was more alarming than that of St Katherine's Priory. The abbot, Robert Hobbes, together with the sexton and sub-prior, held firm in their opposition to the new Protestant practices they had been instructed to introduce. Their consciences would not allow them to accept the claim of the king over that of the pope. A former friar at the abbey and now curate of the local parish church had reported Abbot Hobbes' treachery to the king's officials.

In May 1538 the king's agents arrived at the abbey to take statements from all the monks in positions of importance. Abbot Hobbes together with the sexton and sub-prior remained true to their

Catholic convictions. On 14 June they were tried and found guilty of treason, for which the inevitable punishment was death. Accepting their fates with dignity and bravery, they were hanged, drawn and quartered, protracted and painful ends, the oak tree at the abbey gates used as a gallows. Crowds of people gathered to watch using the steps of the crumbling Queen Eleanor Cross to get a good view of the spectacle. The Cross, once a conduit for the offering of prayers, no longer retained its authority and was now generally regarded as an irrelevance.

Further injunctions imposed yet another tranche of restrictions on the veneration of saints, the cult of relics and displaying of images. It was now decreed that there were to be no candles lighting any image or picture other than the light above the high altar. The candles that had since time immemorial symbolised the light of faith were now extinguished.

Waltham, being a favourite visiting place for King Henry, was the last of the abbeys to be dissolved. It survived until 1540, when its lands were dispersed among the king's favourites.

Similar stories to those of St Katherine's Priory, Woburn and Waltham Abbey were repeated all over the country, as monastic communities were broken up. Many abbey churches became parish churches, such as those at St Albans and Waltham Abbey. Large numbers of monastic buildings fell into ruin. Others were sold or leased by the king, of which many, such as St Katherine's and Delapré Abbey, became private homes. Others continued to be used for social services that had been provided by monks, such as some of the Westminster Abbey buildings which became a school, as did the Lady Chapel of St Albans Abbey. Although much of the fabric of churches and cathedrals remained, their appearance changed drastically, now denuded of the shrines with their bejewelled embellishments. Monastic libraries, containing volumes such as the work of Matthew Paris in St Albans, were broken up, many books irretrievably lost, others removed for the king's personal collection.

THE ELEANOR CROSSES

The sacrament of Mass and the giving of alms at Westminster Abbey on the anniversary of Eleanor's funeral that had been sustained for the 250 years since her death were now terminated, the candles that had burnt continuously around her tomb finally extinguished.

*

After 1547, during the six-year reign of Henry VIII's son and successor Edward VI, the first English monarch to be brought up in the Protestant faith, elimination of the trappings of Catholicism continued apace. Eleanor's tomb at Blackfriars, with its enticing riches, survived until 1550 when the chapel was converted to a parish church and the monuments sold. Royal injunctions ordered the removal of all images, a ruling that led to the destruction of vast quantities of figurative stained glass, defacement of carvings and whitewashing over of representational wall paintings. There was a further cull of such relics as had survived the reign of King Henry. One such loss was the Cross of Neith, which had been such a potent symbol of Edward I's conquest of Wales. After the conquest Edward and Eleanor had taken it with them on many of their travels. This cross was of great significance for subsequent monarchs who used it for the Good Friday act of veneration, approaching it on their knees and barefoot, to show humility and reverence, an act described as 'creeping to the cross'.

The ceremony became increasingly elaborate with the placing of coins on the altar which were made into rings and given to heal those suffering from epilepsy. These practices, which would have been observed by his own father Henry VIII, were banned early in the reign of Edward VI. A few years later the Cross of Neith itself was removed from the chapel at Windsor Castle, along with other sacred treasures, to the Tower of London whence it disappeared without trace.

King Henry had already taken the funds from chantries for the duration of his lifetime and under the new king they were dissolved in their entirety. Although many individual chantries had already lapsed through neglect by this time, the institution remained strong. Now the whole concept of offering Masses for those souls that were suffering the pains of Purgatory was brought to an abrupt end. Chantry priests, such as the incumbent of Queen Eleanor's chantry at Harby, were pensioned off.

*

In spite of the break with the past after King Henry's death the Cheapside Eleanor Cross played a significant role in the coronation of his son, Edward VI, in 1547. It was re-gilded for the occasion, a continuation of a long-standing tradition of using it on ceremonial occasions such as the celebration of Henry V's victory at the Battle of Agincourt in 1415 for which huge numbers of people took part in a re-enactment of the battle. A model castle was constructed and from its gatehouse extended a bridge from which a choir of maidens advanced to meet the king, singing, 'Welcome, Henry the Fifth, King of England and France'.

When the cross began to decay during the fifteenth century a new, even more elaborate monument, rich with gilding and incorporating a drinking fountain, was constructed around it. It consisted of three octagonal stages, each supported by eight slender columns, reaching a height of thirty-six feet. In the first stage stood a statue of a pope, on the second were four apostles, above them the Virgin and child. At the pinnacle was a cross surmounted by a dove.

On Edward VI's death without an heir in 1553, the only surviving child of King Henry VIII and Katherine of Aragon succeeded to the throne, even though female and a Catholic. Queen Mary tried to reverse many of the changes introduced by her father and brother, but so much destruction had taken place that it was impossible to restore the churches to their former glory during the five short years of her reign.

With the accession in 1558 of Elizabeth I, Henry VIII's other daughter, England definitively became a Protestant country although pockets of Catholic dissension persisted. The Cheapside Eleanor Cross, with its elaborate imagery considered as idolising the Virgin Mary, came to be regarded as papist, while for others it continued to be affectionately known as 'The Great Cross in the Cheap'. There were efforts to remove it under the pretext that it obstructed traffic. In one particular night in June 1581 the figures on the lowest stage were vandalised, the arms of the Virgin that held the infant Christ broken, the statue of Edward the Confessor defaced.

The cross was left for the next fourteen years with the broken statue of the Virgin Mary roughly tied to the monument before some repair work was carried out. Around 1596 the figure of the Virgin was replaced with a semi-naked statue of the Roman goddess Diana, water from the Thames flowing from her breasts in mockery of the Catholicism the monument was held to represent. Queen Elizabeth was shocked and ordered that a plain cross should be affixed on the summit and the statue of the Virgin restored. Only twelve nights later her image was vandalised again, her crown knocked off, the sculpture of the baby shattered.

In 1599 there was further discussion about demolishing the cross entirely, described in a sermon at the time as a jewel of the 'Harlot of Rome'. Queen Elizabeth, however, favoured a compromise and ordered that it should be repaired again. Controversial images of saints were replaced with those of apostles, kings and prelates and an iron railing installed to protect it from further attack.

*

This Elizabethan spirit of accord saw the absorption of some of the old religious festivals. As chance would have it the anniversary of the queen's accession day, 17 November, was also the abolished feast day of Hugh of Lincoln, the saint whose intercession Eleanor had sought during the final days of her life. Before its abolition the festival had been customarily celebrated by bell-ringing throughout the diocese of Lincolnshire, then stretching from Lincoln to Oxford, a custom that had in some areas persisted. The tradition now merged imperceptibly into the celebration of Queen Elizabeth as Gloriana, a public holiday on which bells were rung, bonfires lit and ballads sung. While the honouring of saints was now banned, the glorification of monarchy was in keeping with the spirit of the time.

In 1576, reflecting the popularity of drama in the Elizabethan age, the refectory of Blackfriars Monastery where Eleanor's heart tomb had stood until twenty years previously was converted into a theatre. It remained in use until 1584. A new Blackfriars theatre was created from some upstairs rooms of the former monastic buildings in 1596, where William Shakespeare and the King's Men company of actors performed during the winter months, returning to the Globe, on the south bank of the Thames, in the summer.

But for all the triumphs of the reign of Elizabeth her death in 1603 marked the end of the Tudor dynasty. Elizabeth did not leave an heir so the throne of England was offered to James VI of Scotland, who became James I of England, ushering in the Stuart dynasty.

The new king was the son of Mary Queen of Scots, a granddaughter of Henry VIII's sister Margaret and King James IV, the King of Scotland who had been killed by Henry VIII's troops at the Battle of Flodden. The Queen of Scots herself had been a rival to Elizabeth for the throne of England and was executed for plotting to usurp her in 1587. But on Elizabeth's death, Mary's son peaceably became king of the whole of the island of Britain, realising after 300 years Edward I's vision of a unified Britain and ending centuries of hostility between the two nations.

The Eleanor Crosses

Yet under the second Stuart king, Charles, son of James I, the kingdom would be beset by further eruptions of radical upheaval, and once again differences over religious expression would cause damaging rifts. The country was to be torn apart by a bloody civil war, bringing in its train a wave of destruction more significant even than that seen under the Tudor Reformation. The impact on the surviving commemorative legacy of Queen Eleanor was to be immense, as the concept of monarchy itself came under threat.

7.

ELEANOR IN THE CIVIL WAR

The second Stuart King of England and Scotland was a very different monarch from his ancestor, Edward I. King Charles I found himself reaching an impasse with Parliament, an institution that Edward I had done so much to establish. Believing that his MPs were unacceptably infringing his God-given authority, in 1629—four years after his accession—he dispensed with Parliament altogether. Thereafter he sought to govern his kingdom personally, convinced of his divine right to rule.

Inevitably his actions provoked extreme opposition. There was also deep suspicion among the political nation, now largely Protestant, that he wished to bring about a return to Catholicism. The country became deeply divided between the Parliamentarians, who claimed sovereign power for their institution, and the Royalists, who, though they may have had particular grievances against the king, still believed that monarchy was sacrosanct.

By 1642 the country was riven by the Civil War between the supporters of the king and the Parliamentarians. The long years of conflict were violent, with families divided and the damage immense. The destruction brought about by the Civil War was of a scale more sweeping still than the Reformation of the Tudor period, and that done to churches and cathedrals across the country surpassed even the iconoclasm of Edward's reign. Many ecclesiastical buildings, including Westminster Abbey, were used by the Parliamentarians for stabling horses. All frivolous entertainments were now condemned. Blackfriars theatre, one of the casualties, was closed down in 1642 and the buildings demolished in 1655.

THE ELEANOR CROSSES

The form of worship promoted by the Parliamentarians of a puritan persuasion was of a much simpler, more egalitarian nature than the Catholicism of a previous age. There was no place for the trappings of religious expression. At Westminster Abbey wall hangings depicting the life of Christ, given to the Abbey in 1246, were removed in 1644 to adorn the House of Commons and payments were made for 'taking down the angels' and 'cleansing out pictures'. Medieval plate, successfully concealed during the Reformation, was melted down and sold in order to buy horses. Three copes of embroidered velvet made in the twelfth century that were found in the coffin of The Confessor were burned, the salvaged gold given 'to the poor of Ireland'. The painting behind the high altar was stripped of its jewels and precious metals, the oak panel itself used as part of a cupboard, the paintings of the saints hidden from view. William Torel's gilded effigy of Queen Eleanor was a remarkable survival of the stripping out of valuable metal.

The matching effigy in Lincoln Cathedral did not escape. Cartloads of loot were removed. More than two hundred brasses were prised out and many of the tombs destroyed. The bronze figure of Eleanor was taken to be melted down for weaponry.

The effects of the Civil War were keenly felt in the city of London. The Cheapside Cross became the focus of the dispute between the two conflicting sides, with fierce arguments over its fate.

To the anti-Royalist Parliamentarians it was utterly offensive, representing everything they hated about 'Papistry' and the monarchy, hence embodying evil personified, the object of contempt and loathing. It was referred to as 'The Dagon', after the god of the Philistines and it was even proposed that the cross should be convicted of high treason and beheaded. The Committee for Demolition of Monuments to Superstition and Idolatry, the Parliamentary body tasked with rooting out all vestiges of Roman Catholicism, described it as 'sick at heart' and decreed that it was to be demolished. For the supporters of Charles I it was a symbol of the monarchy, a place where they publicly removed their hats and crossed themselves. Parliament issued a warrant for the cross's demolition in 1643, for many occasioning the loss of a much loved landmark.

The demolition of the Cheapside Cross, *Old and New London*, 1887, illustration by Walter Thornbury (Wikimedia Commons).

In the same year the Charing Cross lost its battle to be saved from destruction, by order of the anti-monarchist Parliament. Its loss was later to be lamented in a Cavalier ballad, 'The Downfall of Charing Cross':

> *Undone! undone! the lawyers cry,*
> *They ramble up and down;*
> *We know not the way to WESTMINSTER*
> *Now CHARING-CROSS is down.*
> *Now fare thee well, old Charing-Cross,*
> *Then fare thee well, old stump;*
> *It was a thing set up by a King,*
> *And so pull'd down by the RUMP.*

THE ELEANOR CROSSES

With the loss of the Charing Cross landmark, the reference point traditionally used for the measuring of distances to London from all points of the compass in the kingdom was lost.

The formal destruction of both the Cheapside and Charing Crosses during the Civil War was well publicised. The crosses at Grantham, Stamford, Stony Stratford, Woburn and Dunstable, on the other hand, all disappeared without record during the hostilities, while that at St Albans suffered significant damage. It was fortuitous that the Geddington, Hardingstone and Waltham Crosses survived the onslaughts of the time.

The Parliamentary army was to emerge as the eventual victor in the Civil War with, by the end of 1648, Oliver Cromwell effectively becoming a dictator. During the years of conflict and uncertainty King Charles I was held prisoner in Carisbrooke Castle on the Isle of Wight, remaining a figurehead for any future Royalist uprising.

During his imprisonment people continued to reach out to him through the bars of his cell, seeking the Royal Touch to cure the King's Evil. Though he had lost his freedom the people's belief in his power to cure scrofula, considered to be in the gift of the English monarch since Edward the Confessor, was as strong as ever.

It was essential for Cromwell's purposes that the king should be removed. Charles I was sent to trial for high treason. Clinging to his unshakable view of the divine right of kings, with authority commanded by God and endorsed by the Bible, he refuted the legitimacy of the court. He was found guilty and executed in January 1649. Such a step was deeply shocking, sacrilege to all but a few extreme Parliamentarians. To kill a King of England was certainly not unprecedented, but to do so openly, in a way that claimed justification based on the rule of law, was a drastic break with the past and its belief systems. Whatever his errors of judgement, the king remained to his subjects someone touched by the divine. His death may have removed the man but for some it created a martyr.

A potent cult grew up around him, his execution compared to the Crucifixion. Special powers were attributed to handkerchiefs that were dipped in the king's blood at his beheading. Illustrations in his supposed autobiography, published ten days after his death, even portrayed him with a crown of thorns. Although the ruling faction was successful in killing the king it had failed to kill, and possibly even strengthened, the concept of kingship.

*

For many people the sovereignty of Charles I was considered to automatically transfer to his son, who, as an exile in Holland, became King Charles II. People now sought him out for his gift of being able to cure the King's Evil, with trips arranged for sufferers from England and Scotland across the North Sea to be blessed by his touch.

By 1660 the years of the Protectorate under the rule of Cromwell were over and a triumphant King Charles II was invited back from exile to take up his throne. The Charing Eleanor Cross had by now been levelled but its symbolic significance for the people of London could not be so easily eliminated. The site where it had stood was chosen as the location for a magnificent ceremony to mark the homecoming of the king. After the years of austerity the occasion was one of jubilation, a hugely extravagant affair with a pageant mounted by the king's soldiers in dress uniform.

The site of the Charing Eleanor Cross was also selected for a more gruesome kind of public spectacle. In October 1660 it was here that seven of the surviving signatories of the death warrant of King Charles I who had not escaped abroad were hanged, drawn and quartered. Crowds gathered to cheer as they had the destruction of the Eleanor Cross. Of a more gentle nature, during the early years of reign of Charles II the location was used for a shows of the popular puppet, Puncinello, from southern Italy that was to evolve into Mr Punch of Punch and Judy.

THE ELEANOR CROSSES

The question remained of what permanent use should be made of this site. It so happened that Charles II was offered an imposing bronze statue of his father, the executed Charles I, on horseback. This statue had been commissioned in 1630 by Richard Weston, Lord High Treasurer to Charles I, from the famous French sculptor, Hubert Le Sueur. The first time that an equestrian sculpture had been made of a King of England, it was intended for the garden of Weston's country house, Mortlake Park in Roehampton. To present the king in this way was intended to symbolise the qualities of an invincible leader, an image used in Ancient Rome. King Charles, almost a foot shorter than Edward I had been, was presented as regally imposing, six feet tall in proportion to his horse. The skill of the bronze work was of a standard that would have been acknowledged by William Torel, maker of the effigy of Queen Eleanor. Over life size, the figure of the horse delicately raises up its front leg, the colossal weight of the metal skilfully balanced on the three points of its hooves. By good fortune the sculpture had not been erected by the time of the Civil War and was secreted in the crypt of St Paul's Cathedral, safe from damage by the Parliamentarian army or rampaging mobs.

In 1655, during the years of the Protectorate, the statue was sold by Parliament to John Rivett, a Holborn brazier, with orders to break it up. Rivett took it upon himself to hide the statue, in the hope of selling it at a larger profit. In 1660, following the Restoration, the statue was discovered by Jerome Weston, Second Earl of Portland and eldest son of Richard Weston, still in Rivett's possession. Weston complained to the House of Lords, who decreed that it should be restored to him as its rightful owner. Some years later, in 1675, the statue was bought by Charles II, who ordered that it was to be located on the site of the Charing Eleanor Cross. A carved pedestal of Portland stone, based on a design by Christopher Wren and embellished with the Stuart coat of arms, was made for it. As a symbol of the enduring power of monarchy, King Charles I was placed looking towards Whitehall, the setting of his trial and execution.

Despite the efforts of the Parliamentarians during the Protectorate to obliterate all trappings of kingship, a symbol of royalty had once again taken pride of place, reinstated as one of the official positions from which distances to London are measured. In the words of Edmund Waller, poet and politician, in his 1674 verse 'On the Statue of King Charles I at Charing Cross':

Rebellion, though successful, is but vain,
And kings so kill'd rise conquerors again.
This truth the royal image does proclaim,
Loud as the trumpet of surviving Fame.

King Charles I's statue, Whitehall, unknown artist, c. 1815 (Wikimedia Commons).

During the reign of Charles II the appearance of London did change drastically, though not through deliberate destruction. The devastating Fire of London in 1666 reduced the buildings that would have been familiar to Edward and Eleanor around Cheapside and Cripplegate to ashes, including more than 13,000 houses and eighty-four churches. The old St Paul's Cathedral, where the coffins of both Queen Eleanor and Edward I had rested, and the last remaining parts of Blackfriars Priory were among the losses. Ambitious plans for the rebuilding of the City of London by Christopher Wren were submitted to King Charles. His scheme was not affordable in its entirety, but fifty-one new churches and a new St Paul's Cathedral, its dome revolutionising the London skyline, were built under his direction. The legacy of Eleanor was by now lost from the streets of London.

8.

ELEANOR AND THE ANTIQUARIANS

The sixteenth century saw substantial damage to Eleanor's legacy, with just eight of the twelve crosses surviving. But even while the destruction was taking place the seeds of reclamation of the past were being sown.

From 1539 onwards, John Leland, poet and antiquary to Henry VIII, made a number of journeys around England collecting information about topography and local history. In his notes Leland did not pay much attention to the Eleanor Crosses. His *Itinerary* mentions only one of them, without referring to which medieval queen it commemorates. Leland was, however, greatly interested in Glastonbury Abbey. He identified the nearby hillfort of Cadbury Castle as King Arthur's Camelot, adding further fuel to Tudor fascination with Arthurian mythology.

During the dissolution of the monasteries it was Leland who was responsible for the selection of books from their libraries for the royal collection. One of the works rediscovered was a chronicle written in the 1390s, one hundred years after the death of Eleanor. This account by Thomas Walsingham, a monk from St Albans Abbey, was an iteration of a eulogy to the recently deceased queen, written in 1307. The publication of Walsingham's work did much to rekindle interest in Eleanor among the antiquarians of the sixteenth and seventeenth centuries.

Even as the Civil War was raging there were those who believed that buildings of the past should be respected and recorded. In 1641 a Royalist supporter named Sir Christopher Hatton commissioned

THE ELEANOR CROSSES

Sir William Dugdale to record monuments, inscriptions and stained glass believed to be at risk from damage in violent conflict and from Puritan iconoclasm. The Eleanor Crosses had yet to become regarded as worthy of attention, but it is thanks to Dugdale's *Book of Monuments* that we have a drawing by William Sedgwick of Eleanor's tomb in Lincoln Cathedral with the effigy in place, before it was removed by the Parliamentarians.

Tomb of Eleanor of Castile, from Dugdale's *Book of Monuments* (British Library).

One of the most influential antiquaries was William Camden, whose major study, *Britannia*, was published in 1586. Camden used Leland's notes to inform his own antiquarian studies of the 1570s. He also discovered a description of an attack on Edward when on crusade in the Holy Land in which enemy soldiers managed to trick their way into Edward's presence and stab him with a poisoned knife. The account written fifty years after the event by an Italian chronicler, Ptolemy of Lucca, tells a dubious story about Eleanor herself sucking the poison from Edward's wounded shoulder, thereby saving his life. In *Britannia* Camden brought the accounts of Lucca and Walsingham together with an appreciation of Edward's devotion to her as demonstrated by the crosses, to construct an image of flawless queenly perfection.

The tale of Eleanor's self-sacrifice and wifely dedication in the Holy Land captured the public imagination. It was later taken up, in 1737, by a Scottish poet and playwright named James Thomson, whose main claim to fame was authorship of the lyrics of 'Rule Britannia'. He wrote a highly fanciful dramatisation of the Acre legend in which Eleanor is told by Daraxa, a captive Arab princess, that Edward can be saved if someone sucks the poison from the wound, but will certainly lose their own life. Eleanor passionately begs Edward to allow her to sacrifice herself to save him:

> *'Let me preserve a life, in which is wrapt*
> *The lives of thousands, dearer than my own!*
> *Live thou, and let me die for thee, my Edward!'*

Edward refuses to allow her to die, accepting his own fate, yet she carries out the deed as he sleeps. As she lies dying, the Sultan Selim, impressed by her devotion, enters the camp disguised as a dervish and administers an antidote to the poison. Throughout the play Eleanor is presented as the acme of wifely and motherly duty, an image that was to inform the nineteenth-century view of her, an exemplar of everything a queen consort should be:

> *Whenever woman henceforth shall be praised*
> *For conjugal affection, men will say*
> *There shine the virtues of an Eleanora!*

The Eleanor Crosses

*

By the eighteenth century England was officially a Protestant country with restricted monarchical powers that would have been in many ways unrecognisable to Edward I and Eleanor of Castile. After the destruction of the previous century, only a small proportion now remained of Edward's monuments to his queen. Just one of her three tombs was still in place, while the majority of the crosses were obliterated from the landscape. In St Albans, a town where Parliamentary troops had been quartered during the Civil War, the Eleanor Cross had been left badly damaged. In the mayor's accounts from 1701-02 there is an entry for a sum of money paid for its demolition. It was replaced with a market cross the following year.

Even though the changes that had taken place were far-reaching, much of the magical aura around the monarch that had persisted from the medieval period, through the Tudors and early Stuarts, lingered still. The tradition of the Royal Touch, such a feature of the reign of Edward I, was abandoned after 1689 during the reign of William and Mary as not in keeping with William's strict Calvinist upbringing. Remarkably, it was reintroduced shortly after Queen Anne acceded to the throne in 1702. Her best-known supplicant was the infant Samuel Johnson who was sent to her on the advice of his physician, the eminent Sir John Floyer in 1714. Floyer was not just a proponent of magical healing powers; he was also responsible, among other well respected studies, for ground breaking work in taking measurements of the pulse.

Of the surviving Eleanor Crosses the Hardingstone Cross, now crumbling after years of neglect, fared better than the rest during the early years of the eighteenth century. In 1713, during the reign of Queen Anne, it was restored to mark the end of a conflict that had been raging since 1701, the War of the Spanish Succession. The war had been a massive burden on the British people. Casualties were heavy and the funding of the military campaign had created escalating national debt that in turn limited resources available for peaceable spending at home.

Although the artistic merits of the Eleanor Crosses were still little valued, the concept of courtly love had resonance. The time was now ripe for the restoration of this monument to the devotion between a medieval king and his queen that had long stood forgotten in the English countryside. Stone masons replaced the steps and laid a stone engraved in Latin with words that are translated as:

In everlasting memory of conjugal love the honourable assembly of judges of the county of Northampton resolved to restore this monument to Queen Eleanor when it had nearly fallen down by reason of age in that most auspicious year 1713, in which Anne, the glory of mighty Britain, the most powerful avenger of the oppressed, the arbitress of peace and war, after Germany had been set free, Belgium made secure in her defences, the French overcome in more than ten battles by her own and by the arms of her allies, made an end of conquering and restored peace to Europe after she had given it freedom.

The cross from the summit of the monument had been missing for many years. The masons put in its place a Maltese Cross, with its four arms of equal length, each ending in two sharp straight points. Such a cross, though not in keeping with the aesthetic of the monument, was chosen for the symbolic meaning that it conveyed. Each of its eight points represented one of the obligations of the chivalric knight, obligations, such as to have faith and to love justice, that would have been championed by the nobility at the time of King Edward I. The reputation of Edward I now ran high; he was known as the English Justinian in recognition of his achievements in laying down fundamental principles of law and establishing a meaningful role for Parliament as an associate of the Crown. Loyalty, once considered essential to the bond between magnate and king, was now seen as exemplified in the devotion between King Edward and his queen.

Unfortunately the Geddington Cross was not shown such respect. Having survived the Civil War unscathed, it was badly damaged during the eighteenth century as a result of the local Easter Monday tradition of 'squirrel baiting', which involved catching squirrels in the woods then turning them loose near the cross. The squirrels, in their efforts to escape, would climb up the monument and try to hide among the carving while people pelted them with stones. According to some accounts a live squirrel was tied to the top for the entertainment value of stoning it to death. During the fun much of the decorative moulding was broken off.

The mistreatment of the Geddington Cross aside, the romantic appeal of the Eleanor Crosses gained sway during the eighteenth century. As a result a number of false identifications were made. At Tottenham High Cross, for example, eight miles south of Waltham Cross, there was a wayside cross from which the town derived its name, mentioned in the 1719 travels of the author of *Robinson Crusoe*, Daniel Defoe. It was often thought to have been an Eleanor Cross.

*

In 1717 the Society of Antiquaries of London, which had been meeting informally since 1707, was officially established with the soon-to-be eminent William Stukeley as its president. In 1751 it was given a royal charter to promote 'the encouragement, advancement and furtherance of the study and knowledge of antiquities and history in this and other countries'.

Much of the work of the society concerned the documentation of the standing evidence of the past. The members instituted an ambitious programme of publishing drawings and papers about historical buildings, many of which were generally dismissed as unimportant and irrelevant. Plates were published between 1718 and 1747 when the first of seven volumes of *Vetusta Monumenta* finally appeared. Stukeley was responsible for the drawing of the Waltham Eleanor Cross, an early contribution to the series. His drawing shows in splendid detail the finials, coats of arms and statuary, the cross standing in isolation, an impossibly diminutive man looking up at it.

Stukeley was not typical among the antiquarians in that his fascination with the past embraced the Gothic buildings of the medieval period. Many of the society's members considered Gothic architecture to be the work of barbarians, destroyers of the classical heritage of Ancient Rome. Their interest in Britain's history concerned Roman and pre-Roman studies and did not extend to the recording or preservation of the buildings of the Middle Ages.

On many occasions Stukeley took the stage coach from London to his home in Holbeach, Lincolnshire, the route taking him past the deteriorating monument at Waltham Cross. He was much perturbed by the breakneck speeds at which the coaches rattled past, causing further damage. In spite of opposition from those who despised Gothic architecture, he was able to persuade the members to raise the relatively small sum of money required to construct, in 1721, two protective oak bollards to be set in the road to prevent vehicles driving too close.

Stukeley became vicar of All Saints' Church in Stamford in 1740. He spent much time researching the location of the Eleanor Cross that had been destroyed a hundred years earlier during the Civil War, carefully sifting through records in the town hall for clues. There he found a document published in 1646, almost exactly a century before, by a Richard Butcher, a long forgotten town clerk. This manuscript recorded evidence about then-standing historical monuments, including a description of the Eleanor Cross. He also found a description by a soldier in the Royalist army from 1645, a Captain Symonds. The descriptions had much in common but unfortunately disagreed about the location of the cross.

His research led him to a strange mound of earth, thought by some to be an ancient tumulus. He went to speak to people in that area and although no one could remember there ever having been a cross, locals referred to it as the Queen's Mound, giving strength to the possibility that the monument had stood here. Stukeley, who had carried out significant excavations at Avebury and Stonehenge, dug up the mound. He found a fragment of stone carved in the shape of a flower. The quality and the floral motif reminded Stukeley of the rich patterning on the Geddington memorial cross, twenty miles to the south-east.

He was delighted to be able to report his findings in the local newspaper. He also derived considerable pleasure from the carved rosette which he incorporated into his hermitage, the delightfully ruined grotto he built himself at the bottom of the garden.

Fortunately, elsewhere monuments of the medieval past were being treated with greater respect as interest in the Gothic gathered pace in the late eighteenth century. Richard Gough, director of the Society of Antiquaries from 1771 to 1791, was committed to extending the number of publications relating to Gothic buildings, such as the *Sepulchral Monuments in Great Britain, applied to illustrate the history of families, manners, habits and arts at the different periods from the Norman Conquest to the Seventeenth Century*, published in 1786. In 1789 he published a major work, his additions to *Britannia* in which he expanded Camden's work with his own footnotes. He had considerable respect for Stukeley's work on ancient ruins though he disagreed on many matters. One subject about which they diverged was over the location of the Eleanor Crosses, Gough believing that there were crosses in Harby and Leicester rather than Grantham and Stamford.

Interest in historical subjects among visual artists was strong. Samuel Hieronymus Grimm, a Swiss topographical artist known for his visual recreations of historical events, produced a drawing of the procession from the Tower of London to Westminster for the coronation of Edward VI in 1547. The drawing itself was lost and is now known only through an engraving made of it in 1787 by engraver James Basire. The Cheapside Cross, already destroyed at the time of Grimm's drawing, is prominent in the centre of the image, the road thronged with dignitaries on horseback.

By 1796 interest in the past, as exemplified by the Eleanor Crosses, was significant enough to be the subject of caricature. Cartoonist George Cruikshank used the subject of a group of antiquarians examining the Hardingstone Cross as the subject of a satirical engraving. In this representation the monument has shrunk in size while two open-mouthed gentlemen pore over it and a third rather portly looking man with a riding crop gazes ineffectually towards its upper stages with a microscope.

*

The engraving workshop of James Basire was a thriving concern which, in 1774, received commissions to produce engravings of the tombs of Westminster Abbey for the *Sepulchral Monuments in Great Britain*. At the time Basire was exasperated by constant arguing among his three apprentices in the workshop. The worst of the troublemakers was therefore sent to the abbey to do some sketches from which the engravings would be worked up.

William, the sixteen-year-old apprentice, indeed did some drawing, although even in a largely deserted abbey he managed to pick arguments with noisy pupils from Westminster School who took advantage of this vast space to play skittles. All William wanted was to wander quietly through this treasure chest of English royalty, letting his imagination take him back through the centuries.

Among the tombs was a jumble of waxworks of deceased monarchs, wooden effigies, suits of armour, an attic for centuries of royal death. He felt privileged to be breathing in the dust of history. The elaborate stonework, capitals, bosses, canopies and rib vaults bore faded traces of colour, enough to allow William to imagine the opulence that had existed half a millennium before. He rested his cheek against the vast, austere tomb chest of Edward I, the unforgiving coldness of the marble making him shiver with the reminder of mortality. Its only ornamentation was the Latin text painted on two centuries after the king's death, which translate as 'here lies Edward, I, Hammer of the Scots'.

At the heart of the abbey was the shrine of The Confessor, a glorious Italianate structure raised up on twisted marble columns. The once flat stone floor of the squeezing places, the cramped niches at its base, was worn to smooth troughs from the many years of the sick and blind climbing in to get as close as possible to the holy relics of the saint. For William the aura of the devotion and desperation of the thousands of prayers that had been spoken here was almost palpable.

William sat upon the Coronation Chair itself, constructed to contain the Stone of Scone on which the Kings of Scotland had knelt for their coronations before 1297 when Edward I appropriated it as a trophy to symbolise his domination over the whole island of Britain. For a seat that carried so much significance, it was almost shabby, unimposing, Master Walter of Durham's once bright paintwork now faded. He allowed his thoughts to wander, images of past monarchs, splendid with their coronation robes and jewels, filling his head. His fingers ran over initials of generations of schoolboys, as indifferent to the past as those who angered him now, scratched into the ancient wood. He touched the exposed face of the stone itself, the Stone of Destiny, a crudely shaped grey block blotched with white, no beauty to hint of its significance. Yet this was the very stone described in the Bible on which Jacob laid his head at Bethel in the Holy Land and dreamt of angels ascending a ladder, the link between Heaven and Earth. Jacob set the stone up as a monument and anointed it. His sons took it to Egypt from where it was taken to Spain. Next, still hundreds of years before the birth of Christ, it was taken by invaders to Ireland where it was placed on the holy hill of Tara. From Ireland its journey took it to Scotland, and eventually to the monastery of Scone. There it stayed for four hundred years, the coronation seat for the proud monarchs of Scotland. William's fingertips tingled as he drew them lightly along the cold surface of the sandstone, as if sensing the continuity through the centuries that it embodied.

William felt no disrespect in clambering onto the tombs of deceased royalty in order to draw the effigies, trusting that he did so in the spirit of honouring their legacy. Of the many drawings he made one was of the head of Queen Eleanor from William Torel's bronze effigy. The young apprentice was in awe of the artistry of the long forgotten medieval goldsmith who had achieved a delicacy in bronze that defied the brittleness of the material. William's pencil faithfully reproduced the ripples of hair that seemed to be caught in a moment of swaying in the wind, only the blankness of the eyes detracting from the realism of the figure. The gilt of the bronze remained, as King Edward I intended, untarnished, the office of queen enduring still.

One particular day in early May, William returned to the abbey with the knowledge that he was to be witness to an historic occasion. The warmth of the morning did not penetrate the coolness of the abbey and the atmosphere was hushed as a group of learned antiquarians gathered around the tomb of Edward I in Edward the Confessor's Chapel.

In spite of the objections of some members of the Church, the Society of Antiquaries had been given permission to open the tomb. After the embalming, nearly five centuries before, the tomb had been opened biennially for the subsequent ninety years to renew the wax on the cloth around the body, and the antiquarians were hence curious about its state of preservation. The Dean of the Abbey, John Thomas, was in attendance to ensure that due respect was observed.

Once the seal was broken, it took six strong workmen to lift the solid stone slab from the top of the tomb. Inside it was a smaller coffin, also of marble. Even the most rational of the scholars present could not fail to be affected when its lid was removed and they found themselves looking down on the preserved body of the once powerful king, contained within a recessed cavity. His skin was now brown, almost black, as if he had been exposed to bright sunlight. His rich robes were still intact, in readiness for his coronation on arrival in Heaven. He wore a tunic of red silk damask on top of which was a stole decorated with gilt filigree quatrefoils adorned with glass in shades of red, white, purple and blue, over which lay a web of minute, white, pearl-like beads fixed in place in a complex spiral pattern. His outer garment was a royal mantle of rich crimson satin fastened on the left shoulder with a gilt ring brooch, four inches long, inlaid with red and blue stones. The head of the pin of the brooch was formed by a long piece of transparent blue paste, shaped like an acorn, seed of the mighty oak, suggesting the strength of the royal dynasty.

In his right hand the king held a sceptre, two and a half feet in length, surmounted by a cross of gilded copper. In his left was a sceptre five and a half feet long, decorated with three tiers of oak leaves in green enamel, topped with a dove of white enamel, as had long been emblematic of English kings. On his head was a crown of a gilded tin-like metal, decorated with trefoils. There were no rings on his fingers, even though they were a customary sign of royalty. The antiquarians deduced that over the centuries the king's fingers had shrunk and the rings fallen off into his garments. Out of respect, no attempt was made to find them. On the backs of his hands were gold quatrefoils, it being assumed that these were fixed onto gloves of linen so fine that the fabric had turned to dust. The antiquarians took careful measurements of the king. They found him to be six foot two inches tall, well deserving of his nickname, Longshanks. This man was every inch a king, dressed for coronation, as he was to be received on judgement day.

William was mesmerised by the proceedings, at first unable to respond, moved that so much trouble should be taken to dress the body of someone to be entombed. Realising he was, at his young age, privileged to be party to such a momentous occasion, he determined to make a record of his impressions. He dashed down two sketches, but to draw the features of the long dead king seemed disrespectful. He simplified the shapes, rendering the faceless body flat, contained within the lozenge of the coffin. He was able to capture a sense of the size of this huge man, his shoulders seeming almost too big for their container. There was no time for further reflection; after an hour the dean was insistent that enough was enough and the tomb was resealed, its contents untouched. Prayers were said for the soul of the king, forgiveness asked for this rough invasion of his tomb. In order to ensure that King Edward was never disturbed again, molten pitch was poured into the tomb to cover the body before it was resealed. The Society of Antiquaries was presented with a drawing by James Basire of Edward in his coronation robes, based on notes and sketches made on the occasion.

William also sketched the face from the effigy of Edward III, Eleanor's grandson, now lying on the opposite side of The Confessor's Chapel. His wise looking head, the frown lines on his forehead delicately picked out, the stiffly flowing hair and beard were to provide him with a lasting image of a venerable old man. William knew that this much-revered king had held his grandfather in high regard, sending the monks of the abbey costly gold cloth to cover his tomb. Like the grandparents he had never met, the third King Edward was passionate about Arthurian legend, even calling his second son Lionel after one of Arthur's Knights of the Round Table.

As he stood in Edward the Confessor's Chapel surrounded by the tombs of the Plantagenet monarchs, William was aware that he might have been standing on soil that was once walked on by Christ himself. The floor was raised a full six feet above the level of the rest of the church, set into earth from the Holy Land that was taken in shiploads hundreds of years ago to Italy, whence it was sent to England. He would surely have remembered that soil more than thirty years later, when this boy who became the famous William Blake wrote the words to 'Jerusalem':

And did those feet in ancient time.
Walk upon England's mountains green

For William Blake the formative experiences of his work in Westminster Abbey were to go deep, contributing to his love of the spirituality of a neglected medieval past that was to inform the bulk of his prolific career. His dislike of 'copying nature', drawing instead upon his imagination, was not in keeping with the prevailing spirit of his time. When he was over sixty years old, around 1819, he found encouragement in the friendship of an artist and astrologer called John Varley. Varley, who believed himself to have revelatory gifts, was regarded as a complete eccentric. With the encouragement of his friend, Blake produced dozens of 'visionary heads', sketches of historical characters who presented themselves in his imagination during their night-time sessions as if sitting for portraits. One such drawing of a Queen Eleanor could be that of Eleanor of Aquitaine, consort of Henry I, rather than Eleanor of Castile. But this portrait is most likely to have been inspired by his image from all those years earlier of the effigy of Eleanor of Castile, visualised with eyes gazing heavenwards in humble devotion.

William Blake, Visionary Head of Queen Eleanor (Wikimedia Commons).

THE ELEANOR CROSSES

More outlandish is the image Blake produced of 'The Assassin Lying Dead at the Feet of Edward I in the Holy Land'. This creature looks barely human, its hair and beard giving it the appearance of some sort of primitive lion. Perhaps Blake's views on physiognomy, that a person's innate qualities determine his outward appearance, encouraged him to bring out the animal in a man who attempted to murder the king of England. Although controversial in his time, Blake's impact on literature and the visual arts during the later nineteenth century and beyond was enormous. It was partly through him and his followers that a popular fascination with medievalism was to take hold and with it a revival in Gothic architecture. During the age of the Victorians the composition of an Eleanor Cross was to become a model for memorial architecture, while Eleanor herself would be safely assured of her place as the epitome of what a queen consort should be. The legacy King Edward intended for Queen Eleanor was to live on, though the form it was to take would have been unimaginable to him.

9.

ELEANOR IN THE GOTHIC REVIVAL

Augustus Welby Northmore Pugin, a hugely prolific architect whose work started around 1830, was obsessed with everything Gothic. He drove himself to unsustainable limits and, following a complete nervous breakdown, died in 1852 at the age of forty. For Pugin the Gothic represented the true expression of Christianity, which for him meant Catholicism. During his curtailed career he produced a vast number of faithfully detailed drawings recording Gothic architectural and decorative forms as well as designing large numbers of neo-Gothic buildings.

His influence in popularising the Gothic style was enormous. When in 1838, during the construction of the London sewer system, two fragments of heraldic shields from Michael of Canterbury's original Eleanor Cross at Cheapside were found, they were now regarded as worth preserving and became the property of the Corporation of London.

The establishment of neo-Gothic architecture was aided by a massive fire in 1834 that destroyed virtually all the medieval Palace of Westminster, by then home to the Houses of Commons and Lords. St Stephen's Chapel and the work of Michael of Canterbury, which had been commissioned by Edward I, were among the losses. The blaze was watched by thousands, some cheering the sweeping away of the past, including Charles Dickens and the painters JMW Turner and John Constable. The fire started in a stove in the basement in which workmen, under the instruction of the Clerk of Works, were burning cartloads of wooden sticks on which government accounts had been notched from Norman times until the practice was discontinued in 1826.

A competition was held to select a new design, the award going to the neo-Gothic proposal of architect Charles Barry, whose building now dominates the north bank of the Thames by Westminster. Details and interior designs, right down to furnishings, are the work of Pugin, whose casing for the clock, Big Ben, surmounts Barry's tower.

Nine years later, in 1843, a competition was held for the design of frescos for the new House of Lords. This was won by William Dyce whose scenes based on Arthurian legends evoke an ideal of monarchy and nationhood, continuing the enthusiasms of Eleanor and Edward.

Pugin provided inspiration to the most prolific architect of the Gothic Revival, George Gilbert Scott. One of Gilbert Scott's creations was the Martyrs' Memorial in Oxford, completed in 1843, its design based on the Waltham Eleanor Cross, which had itself been restored a decade earlier. The history of the Martyrs' Memorial is rooted in passionate theological discussion that was then raging in Oxford. A group of Oxford Anglican theologians was deeply concerned that the rival Tractarian movement was moving alarmingly close to Catholic practices in religious expression, pointing to excessive use of trappings such as candles, incense, elaborate vestments and statuary. The Anglicans were determined to counter this trend by commissioning a memorial to the three Protestant martyrs who were burned at the stake in Oxford during the reign of the Catholic Queen Mary in 1555 and 1556. The Martyrs' Memorial Committee was therefore established in 1838. The plaque on the completed monument states that the martyrs died,

> bearing witness to the sacred truths which they had affirmed and maintained against the errors of the Church of Rome.

Ironically, even though the original function of an Eleanor Cross was rooted in Catholicism, its form was now being used to commemorate those Protestant martyrs who died for their opposition to the Church of Rome.

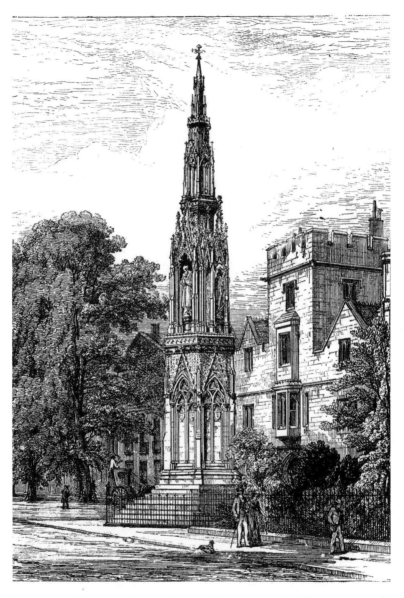

Late-nineteenth-century drawing of Martyrs' Memorial, Oxford (From Old Books).

THE ELEANOR CROSSES

While the Martyrs' Memorial was under construction the Hardingstone Eleanor Cross was restored again. The architect Edward Blore removed 'various 18th century accretions', replacing the Maltese Cross with a rather incongruous broken classical column.

The Ilam Cross (R J Higginson/Wikimedia Commons).

The shape of an Eleanor Cross was to influence the design of numerous other memorial structures. One particular memorial was built in 1840 by the landowner and Conservative MP Jesse Watts-Russell at Ilam Hall in Staffordshire for his wife Mary. Watts-Russell, knowing of Gilbert Scott's work on the Martyrs' Memorial, decided to base the memorial to his wife on the design of an Eleanor Cross, commissioning a now less well remembered architect, John Macduff Derick, to carry out the work.

There are some striking parallels between Mary Watts-Russell and Eleanor: Mary died at the age of forty-eight, just a year younger than Eleanor, leaving eight children, while Eleanor left six. Both left grief-stricken husbands who were driven to commemorate them in stone. But for Jesse Watts-Russell the purpose of the cross was simply to commemorate a lost love, the inscription reading that it was erected by him in order to 'perpetuate the memory of one who lives in the hearts of so many in this village and neighbourhood'. The concept of establishing a relationship with a departed soul, the motivation that inspired Edward I, would have been completely alien to the Protestant Watts-Russell.

The Martyrs' Memorial was also used as the basis of a design of a new monument at Charing Cross where a railway station began operations in 1864. The station's grand hotel, designed by Edward Middleton Barry, son of Charles Barry, the designer of the Palace of Westminster, was opened the following year. The hotel owners were, of course, keen to attract customers after the significant investment they had made and set out to make the hotel a new landmark for London. They came up with a scheme to use the historic significance implied in the very name of the station to create their own monument. The area, formerly the village of Charing, long since absorbed into the city of London, had for many years been referred to as Charing Cross after the long gone Eleanor Cross. Unconcerned that they did not have ownership of the true location of the Eleanor Cross, now graced by the statue of Charles I, they determined to create an Eleanor Cross as the centrepiece to the station forecourt.

THE ELEANOR CROSSES

In the fashion of the time they imagined a work of Gothic splendour, Victorian-style, replete with finials, four centred arches, shafts of coloured marble, gloriously carved excrescences, to sit alongside their French Renaissance-style hotel. Little expense was spared for the building of the monument which rises to seventy feet, terminating in a spire and cross. No fewer than eight statues of Queen Eleanor still look down on the bustling crowds outside the station.

Charing Cross hotel and monument (1872), *The London Illustrated News.*

A proliferation of monuments was to spring up across the country, many of which are approximately reminiscent of an Eleanor Cross. The existing cross at Banbury in Oxfordshire, as remembered in the nursery rhyme, is one such example. It was built by architect John Gibbs in 1859 to replace earlier crosses destroyed by the Puritans in the seventeenth century. In this case it was not to commemorate death but the marriage of Queen Victoria's eldest daughter to Prince Frederick of Prussia.

The Banbury Cross, c. 1895 (Wikimedia Commons).

During the Victorian era there was a flurry of restoration of many medieval Gothic buildings, though opinions differed widely regarding how such work should be carried out. Gilbert Scott had a hand in restoration work in hundreds of churches and cathedrals across the country, including St Albans Abbey and Westminster Abbey, and was responsible for much ruthless stripping out and replacement of work not considered suitably in keeping with the whole. He believed that by replacing original stone with new, replicating authentic Gothic forms, buildings could be returned to their former beauty and their true state. For others the replacement of old stone with new was unacceptable. John Ruskin, the leading art critic and painter active from around 1840, was enormously influential in the school of thought that opposed modern interference with the ancient. In the winter of 1871-72 he produced a collection of drawings and casts of details in Westminster Abbey, intended as technical illustrations to aid students at the School of Drawing that he had established in Oxford. His drawing of the arms of the county of Ponthieu from Queen Eleanor's tomb lovingly records every detail of the fragile stone, the damage to the top right corner and the bottom tip, painstakingly reproduced.

John Ruskin, Study of the Form of a Shield, from the Tomb of Eleanor of Castile in Westminster Abbey (Ashmolean Museum).

Although there were wide discrepancies in their views on how the architecture of the past should be respected Gilbert Scott and Ruskin worked together on findings at St Albans Abbey, where Gilbert Scott was employed to undertake the restoration. From the sixteenth century the Lady Chapel of the abbey had been blocked off from the rest of the building and used to house the town's Grammar School. The space was filled with rows of wooden desks on which generations of pupils had carved their names. The beautiful carvings of forgotten medieval masons had been badly damaged by bored schoolboys, the arcading on the walls concealed by wooden panels. In 1868 work began on removing the fittings of the school and opening up the blocked arches that separated it from the rest of the church.

To the delight of Gilbert Scott, much of the masonry that was being used as infill was found to consist of pieces of carved and painted Purbeck marble and limestone. He was convinced he had found the fragments of the long lost shrines to St Alban and St Amphibalus, destroyed during the Reformation. The workmen began the painstaking task of reassembling the damaged pieces, only to be criticised for wasting time and money by members of the Restoration Committee who did not subscribe to such Catholic practices as worship of saints. Gilbert Scott gained the support of Ruskin, who considered the discovery of the shrines to be of national importance and offered to pay for their reconstruction himself. The national newspapers were alerted to the discovery and the restoration did indeed take place.

*

In 1851 the Museum of Manufactures was founded in London. In the spirit of Victorian eclecticism it set out to display all forms of decorative art from all periods alongside fine art to present a more rounded picture of artistic endeavour than in previous public galleries. This nineteenth-century concept was something of a return to the medieval aesthetic, with all art forms, including sculpture, painting, metal and woodwork, valued for their decorative qualities that contributed to a whole sensory experience. Alexander of Abingdon did not create his statues for display in isolation, nor would Walter of Durham have understood his paintings removed from their context and placed in a frame.

In 1862, thirty-five mosaic images of European artists and designers were commissioned to decorate the south court of a museum then known as the South Kensington Museum. The sequence, known as the Kensington Valhalla, included portraits of notable artists such as Leonardo da Vinci and Raphael, and also craftsmen such as the English wood carver Grinling Gibbons, in recognition of the growing belief in the connection between fine and applied arts. Significant artists of the day were commissioned to produce the designs. William Torel, creator of the bronze effigies of Eleanor, was selected as part of the pantheon to represent metalwork.

The mosaic was based on a design by Richard Burchett (1815-75), creator of a number of Tudor-era portraits and paintings of the Spanish Armada for the House of Lords in the Palace of Westminster. With no record of what Torel looked like, the image is entirely fanciful, a heavily bearded Victorian gentleman in period costume standing in front of Eleanor's tomb in Westminster Abbey, an Eleanor Cross in the background.

The foundation stone for a new building to house the expanding collection of the South Kensington Museum was laid in 1899 by Queen Victoria, the occasion used to change its name to the Victoria and Albert Museum by which it continues to be known.

Even though Victorian architecture fell out of fashion and much was lost during developments of the 1960s and 1970s, there are still many examples all around us. It is thanks to them and their embracing of the Gothic as the building style of default that the Eleanor Cross formation may even now seem so familiar.

10.

ELEANOR IN THE LAST
HUNDRED YEARS

At the outbreak of the Second World War in 1939 Kenneth Clark, then director of the National Gallery, brought attention to aspects of the conflict that could easily have been overlooked: the threat of damage to the landscape and buildings of Britain and concern about the livelihood of artists.

His views were much in the spirit of those of Sir Christopher Hatton, originator of the *Book of Monuments* at the outset of the Civil War in the seventeenth century. Both were driven by the importance of recording the physical environment in the event of possible destruction. For Clark the endeavour was also concerned with harnessing the subjectivity of artistic interpretation, rather than simply accurate documentation.

Clark proposed a scheme for artists to record the 'changing face' of Britain to the Pilgrim Trust, a charity funded by an American billionaire. The programme, which was to become known as *Recording Britain*, was established under the guidance of a steering committee. The emphasis was very much on using visual artists, predominantly painters, to record aspects of British topography and building stock that may not have been regarded as of national importance, but were considered to be at risk. Perceived threats included German invasion, Britain's own defensive manoeuvres or simply the pace of modern development.

Typical subjects selected were market towns and villages, parish churches and country estates, rural landscapes and industries, monuments and ruins. Of the chosen artists, some were well known, others relatively unfamiliar. One of the scenes was the Eleanor Cross in Geddington, painted in watercolour by Stanley Roy Badmin in 1940. The tranquillity of the view is disturbed by the unsettling figures of two men in military uniform walking past the monument.

Of the Eleanor Crosses that remained at the outset of the war the one potentially most at risk was at Waltham Cross. During the hostilities the Royal Gunpowder Mills, less than a mile from the site of the cross, were important in the production of explosives, and the town therefore became a target for German air attack. The first bombs fell on Waltham Cross in September 1940, causing significant damage to buildings but no loss of life. In 1941 the town lost most of its medieval buildings that had been clustered around Romeland where Henry VIII had owned property.

The most serious incident in terms of loss of life was on 12 August 1944 when an American B-24 Liberator crashed just outside the town. Members of the Auxiliary Fire Service arrived to a scene of devastation, with debris scattered far and wide. Among the scattered, twisted pieces of metal were burned body parts and fragments of clothing. Young volunteers were told to collect up the pieces and put them in individual heaps as best they could. The Land Girls working the fields continued to find human remains for months afterwards.

It later became known that ten American airmen died that night, having bravely steered their plane away from the town to avoid civilian casualties. The events of a few moments were to leave ten families from the other side of the Atlantic torn apart with grief. Pilot John Ellis from California was one of the young men who died. He was given a burial of sorts in the American Cemetery in Cambridge. A memorial plaque was put up in Cheshunt Public Library, a few miles from Waltham Cross, inscribed with his and the other crew members' names.

In March 1945 there were losses among civilians when a V2 rocket fell in the centre of town. Three children were killed, eleven-year-old Audrey Clark and her four-year-old brother Norman, and eight-year-old James Strudwick. In total there were five fatalities and fifty-three injuries. Two days later there was another air attack leading to two further deaths.

Remarkably, in spite of sixteen long range rockets, fourteen flying bombs, fifteen parachute mines, thirty containers of incendiary bombs and 500 other types of bomb that fell on the town of Waltham Cross during the course of the war, the Eleanor Cross remained standing, only its terminal cross lost due to the vibration of the bombs. The greatest extent of the damage to the monument was in fact caused by the track arms of the trolley buses which provided the passenger service from Waltham Cross to London as they swung loose from the overhead wires when turning the corner.

Of all the losses inflicted in the war, the remaining Eleanor memorials were not among them, leaving three crosses still standing into the twenty-first century.

*

Of the original twelve Eleanor Crosses only those at Geddington, Hardingstone and the heavily restored Waltham Cross remain, now Grade I listed buildings. After the Second World War, even though no longer at risk from bomb damage, the Waltham Cross was restored and the statues replaced with replicas. The originals were removed for safekeeping and were put on display in Cheshunt Library. They were loaned to the Victoria and Albert Museum where they are now in storage.

A few fragments of the lost crosses survive. One of the statues from the Lincoln cross can be seen in the grounds of Lincoln Castle. A carved stone flower, allegedly a fragment from the Stamford Cross that was excavated in William Stukeley's garden, is on display in the town's public library. The fragments of the Cheapside Cross showing the arms of England and Castile which were found during the construction of a sewer can now be seen in the Museum of London.

Detail of Hardingstone Cross (Polipholo/Wikimedia Commons).

Eleanor in the Last Hundred Years

Eleanor's tomb in Westminster Abbey, with the bronze effigy made by William Torel, remains in situ, opposite the shrine of Edward the Confessor. There is also a replica of the statue in the Victoria and Albert Museum. The effigy on her tomb in Lincoln Cathedral is a replica dating from 1891, the original having been one of the casualties of the Civil War. Richard Burchett's mosaic depicting William Torel, creator of the effigies, is also in storage at the Victoria and Albert Museum.

Eleanor's heart tomb at Blackfriars Priory was destroyed in the aftermath of the dissolution of the monasteries without any visual record having been made of it and any surviving monastic buildings were lost in the Fire of London of 1666. Blackfriars is now remembered in the name of a bridge and a London tube station. The theatre of Elizabethan times survives only in the name of Playhouse Yard on which it stood.

The equestrian statue of Charles I, on the site of the destroyed Charing Cross, remains standing. It is now overlooked and overshadowed by Nelson's Column, the ornate marble pedestal pitted and crumbling, the detail of Wren's original design indistinct. It stands in isolation, cut off from the pedestrianised area of Trafalgar Square by a busy road. Although its location is no longer a focal point, it continues to be one of the measuring points for distances to London.

There are very few survivals of the relics and artefacts that were such an important part of the expression of faith at the time of Edward and Eleanor after their systematic destruction during the Protestant Reformation. Only a small proportion is left of medieval metalwork, the reliquaries and chalices, patens and chrismatories, the materials too valuable and easily removed for melting down. Some examples can be seen in museums, completely dissociated from the context for which they were intended. Many of the artefacts that are now on view avoided destruction as they were deliberately hidden during the Reformation.

The medieval crown and royal regalia of England, likely to have dated from the coronation of Edward the Confessor in 1042, were broken up in the seventeenth century when the country was under the rule of Oliver

Cromwell. It is possible that some parts were preserved by priests of Westminster Abbey and are inset into the present crown, which is still referred to as St Edward's Crown. The anointing spoon that was used in the coronation of Edward I and Eleanor, dating from 1200, survives and was used in the 1953 coronation of Elizabeth II. The structure of the coronation ceremony then conducted was very similar to that of the time of Edward I and Eleanor, which in itself was modelled on that of King Edgar and Queen Ælfthryth in 973. Westminster Abbey itself has been used for royal coronations since that of King Harold in 1066.

We are now left with a few tantalising glimpses into the riches of the medieval Church. The painting that was behind the high altar in Westminster Abbey was a remarkable survival. Stripped of its valuable inlaid jewels it was spared destruction as it was a useful large piece of oak. It was rediscovered in 1725 by the antiquarian, George Vertue, being used as the top of a cupboard housing funeral effigies. Edward Blore, restorer of the Hardingstone Eleanor Cross, again rediscovered it in 1827 and made efforts to preserve it in a glass fronted frame. Thought to be Britain's oldest surviving oil painting, with its central image of St Peter holding the key to the kingdom of heaven, it is considered to be the finest late-thirteenth-century painting in northern Europe. Since 1998 it has undergone further restoration.

Of the Eleanor Crosses themselves, even though only three of the twelve originals remain, their creation has had a pronounced impact on our physical environment. Monuments with several narrowing tiers, frequently decorated with pointed Gothic arches and finials and much loved by the Victorians, can be seen in towns and cities across the country. Thousands of people must pass the monument outside Charing Cross station in London on a daily basis without giving it a second glance, though David Gentleman's murals along the platform of the Northern line depicting the building of the original cross serve as a reminder of the connection to Eleanor.

*

Eleanor in the Last Hundred Years

While the extent of Eleanor's influence on Edward's decision making and the subsequent course of English history is unknown, it is acknowledged that her commemorative legacy holds a significant place in the story of the development of English Gothic architecture. The ogee arch, formed by the intersection of two curves that sweep from concave at the bottom to convex at the top was used for the first time in the Eleanor Crosses and gave rise to a vast expansion of the repertoire of available ornamental patterns. The building of the crosses has been described as a key stage in the history of English architecture, an evolutionary shift after which nothing was quite the same again.

The two-centred pointed arch of earlier forms of Gothic architecture was now embellished with the introduction of the four-centred arch, giving a reverse curve where the flow of the line changes direction. This development in Gothic architecture, an elaboration of the style now aptly named Decorated, is noted for its love of elegantly flowing curves, the serpentine line.

The range of patterns that the ogee arch made possible gave rise to endless possibilities. Used to great effect in window tracery patterns, the narrow bars of stone that are used to decorate the head of the arch create shapes that are reminiscent of flames, teardrops, hearts, daggers, in any number of combinations.

While the first modest beginnings of the ogee arch in England were seen in the Eleanor Crosses, they reached their full manifestation in buildings such as the Lady Chapel of St Albans Abbey, completed in 1327. In Ely Cathedral, completed in 1349, there is a further delightful innovation with the arches also curving forwards, a nodding ogee arch. The aesthetic of this style of architecture is highly likely to have been influenced by Islamic motifs that were seen by the Crusaders, including Eleanor herself, and in the Moorish architecture of southern Spain.

This spirited experimentation with delightfully varied, curvaceous architectural forms that characterised the Decorated period of the early fourteenth century, also referred to as curvilinear, was relatively short-lived. Decorated architecture was superseded in about 1350 by the

THE ELEANOR CROSSES

Perpendicular, the final phase of Gothic architecture when variety was replaced by regularity, curves by straight, grid-like lines. It is perhaps no coincidence that the stylistic change from Decorated to Perpendicular Gothic occurred shortly after the devastation of the Black Death, which struck in 1348. The disease led to a drastic fall in the population, a consequent reduction in the workforce available for building projects and a sharp increase in labour costs, all factors that perhaps contributed to the limitation of the repertoire in building styles.

In the heyday of the Gothic Revival the Victorians came to regard the Decorated style, with its love of flowing linear pattern, as the great achievement of medieval Gothic architecture. Its architectural forms, as interpreted by the Victorians, are now ubiquitous in ecclesiastical and civic building.

The aesthetic that was introduced in the Eleanor Crosses was not restricted to architecture but also extended across the visual arts. The drawings and paintings of William Blake were much influenced by his early studies of the art of the Middle Ages, with his distinctive flat, linear imagery and the 'flaming line' of the undulating curves that characterise his work.

For Blake it was the spirit of medieval art and not just the style in which it was manifested that spoke to him. The art of the Middle Ages provided, he believed, a link to an English Arcadia, a utopian view of a past that was rich in mystical symbolism. Like the medieval artists he took inspiration from, Blake was not seeking accurate representation of a physical world. Rather than basing his work on observation, he relied upon his inner eye, a world of imagination. Such a rejection of the accepted standards of the time was considered shocking but his work was to be a source of inspiration to many later artists, channelled through the work of his disciple, Samuel Palmer. His influence continued through to the twentieth century, to be seen in the works of painters such as Paul Nash and Graham Sutherland. The paintings of these neo-Romantic artists are infused with a spirit that draws upon the past, inviting the viewer to imagine forgotten landscapes.

ELEANOR IN THE LAST HUNDRED YEARS

*

It was a love of medieval art and disillusionment with the modern world that led, in 1848, to the formation of the Pre-Raphaelite Brotherhood. The seven original members, including artist and poet Dante Gabriel Rossetti, acknowledged a debt to the rich internal imagination of Blake that looked back to the medieval past. They and their followers believed that with the growing sophistication and polish of the Renaissance the purity of vision of the Middle Ages was lost.

The Pre-Raphaelite vision was to widen out from the founding close-knit group to inform the loosely termed Aesthetic Movement. Its proponents regarded true beauty as paramount and upheld the value of 'art for art's sake', an aesthetic concept that would have been unintelligible to the creators of the Gothic cathedrals. The Pre-Raphaelite sensibility was to go on to permeate the Arts and Crafts Movement. A key figure was William Morris who, together with Pre-Raphaelite artists Dante Gabriel Rossetti and Edward Burne-Jones, decorated the walls and ceiling of the library in Oxford University's Union building with scenes from Arthurian legend. As well as embracing the aesthetic of the Middle Ages, Morris reviled the age of the machine and advocated a return to manual techniques. Medieval crafts that had been largely forgotten fascinated him. He personally mastered the forgotten art of tapestry, using natural dyes and hand weaving, re-discovering methods that would have been available in the thirteenth century.

The Arts and Crafts movement was in turn to feed into Art Nouveau design of the early twentieth century, an aesthetic that extended into all aspects of craftsmanship. Characterised by its love of luxuriant curves and sweeping lines, the distinctive contours of Art Nouveau are those that were tentatively used in the Eleanor Crosses.

Arthurian imagery, which had been so powerful for Edward and Eleanor, in part derived from the twelfth-century writings of Geoffrey of Monmouth and persisted with ever greater elaboration throughout the later medieval and Tudor periods. The Pre-Raphaelites were fascinated by Arthurian legend and the chivalric values it represented. It was the tales of King Arthur, as told by the fifteenth-century writer Thomas Malory, which Rossetti and friends chose to illustrate in the murals of the Oxford Union, begun in 1857. Arthuriana also crossed the Atlantic, aided by *Camelot*, a popular 1960 musical, with the song lyric: 'Don't let it be forgot, that once there was a spot, for one brief shining moment, that was known as Camelot.' John F. Kennedy was a fan of the musical, according to his widow Jacqueline, and the name was admiringly attached to the short-lived glamour of his presidency. Even today, the enduring fascination with King Arthur persists as strongly as ever. Indeed, Arthur Uther Pendragon, neo-Druid leader, eco-campaigner and scourge of English Heritage, regards himself as the reincarnation of King Arthur.

*

The lasting appeal of the Eleanor Crosses exceeds their significance as an interesting development in the history of art. They also tell a story of survival and continuity that is exemplified by the endurance of the institution of monarchy. The role of a medieval king was not an easy one. He was expected to be strong and decisive while acting within the rule of law and in consultation with the nobility. Failure to rule adequately could lead to intervention from the magnates, whether through the imposition of concessions as in the case of the Magna Carta, or violent usurpation of power. Even a king with a reputation for strength such as Edward I came close to facing revolt in 1297. Accused of mismanaging negotiations with France over control of Gascony, he was forced to make a humble appeal to his past successes in order to reassert his position of authority.

Edward I intended the Eleanor Crosses to remind the people of the enduring power of monarchy. Its continuing survival is a success story of extraordinary magnitude that has at times seemed far from secure. The history of the succession bristles with stories of violent upheaval. Numerous individual monarchs have met untimely ends, whether murdered (Edward II), declared unfit to rule (Henry VI), killed fighting for their crown (Richard III) or executed (Charles I). In the Middle Ages rules governing male primogeniture were not as rigidly established as they are today and matters of succession were often hotly disputed. Examples of the killing of rival claimants to the throne are many, the likely murder of the Princes in the Tower by their uncle, thereby ensuring his position as Richard III, perhaps being the most infamous.

While the ancestral thread between William the Conqueror and Queen Elizabeth II can be traced, it is marked by significant discontinuities. The Royal House of Windsor is the product of innumerable chance occurrences, even allowing for exclusions from the royal line of succession through illegitimacy, being female or Catholic.

Uncertainties around entitlement to the throne have served to give weight to the ritual of the coronation ceremony. The acts of crowning and anointing with holy oil are of momentous symbolic importance, giving legitimacy to the incumbent's right to reign. There are several examples of dashes to Westminster to be crowned where there could have been doubts over the succession. It is not insignificant that Edward I felt sufficiently secure in his entitlement to the throne that his joint coronation with Eleanor did not take place until over two years after he became king.

As Henry III intended, Westminster Abbey continues to embody the concept of royalty, still used for symbolic royal occasions, coronations, weddings and funerals. The oak Coronation Chair, commissioned by Edward I in 1296 and used in every coronation since 1399, has in recent years been restored and is now preserved behind a glass screen. Beneath its seat is an empty space that previously housed the Stone of Scone. The iconic stone was finally returned to Scotland in 1996 with the intention that it would remain there until temporarily returned to Westminster for the coronation of the next monarch of a united Britain.

THE ELEANOR CROSSES

In a world where the functions of monarchy have changed dramatically, the symbols and language that surround it persist. The heir apparent to the monarch is still described as the Prince of Wales, a term that has its antecedence in the birth of the son of Edward I at Caernarvon Castle in north-west Wales. The aura around the monarchy continues to exert an elusive, indefinable power. One way in which that power was manifested as late as 1714 was in the ritual of the Royal Touch. On that occasion the alleged possession of that curative gift was used as evidence of the authenticity of a claim to the throne, in the case of James, Duke of Monmouth, illegitimate son of Charles II. Although the ritual did not survive the death of Queen Anne and the arrival of the Hanoverian kings, people still seek proximity to royalty. Crowds flock just to get a glimpse of the present queen and other members of the royal family. Young children turn out to press bunches flowers onto visiting royals, even royals by marriage such as the Duchess of Cambridge.

No other member of the English royal family before or since has received such an extensive memorial legacy as that created by Edward I for Eleanor. Not even Queen Victoria's extensive commemoration of Prince Albert after she was widowed in 1861 can rival it. She commissioned George Gilbert Scott to design the Albert Memorials in both London's Hyde Park and in Albert Square, Manchester. He took his inspiration from the Eleanor Crosses, which he described as the most touching monuments ever erected to a royal consort. Like the Eleanor Crosses he wished to give the structures 'the character of a vast shrine, enriching it with all the arts by which the character of preciousness can be imparted ... and which it can be made to express the value of the object it protects.' His description encapsulates how the original Eleanor Crosses with their elaborate stone work, resplendent with rich colour and sparkling with gilt, would have appeared in the thirteenth century. At a time when only the few had more than the most basic of possessions, the richness of the structure would have reinforced the concept of royalty as sacred.

The Albert Memorial, London (Photo by DAVID ILIFF. License: CC-BY-SA 3.0).

While the Eleanor Crosses were powerful testimonials to the importance of the office of kingship, they were also physical statements of the devotion that Edward I, the man, felt towards his wife and queen. They represent emotional bonds that resonate across the centuries. They served as reminders that though the king was somehow imbued with the Holy Spirit he was, like his subjects, a man with human passions.

For King Edward to commission three separate tombs for Eleanor was revealing of the privilege enjoyed by a few, but multiple burials were not unknown. To us today the concept of having three separate burial places for a loved one seems strange, even ghoulish. Even at the time it was a practice discouraged by the Church, conflicting with the prevailing view that the body should be kept whole, ready for the day of final judgement. Yet in spite of the teaching of the Church there was a strong motivation for the division of the bodies of saints. The wide distribution of these relics among religious foundations allowed many more of the faithful to access them and connect with their souls through prayer as well as providing a lucrative trade.

Some of the bones of St Alban, for example, were taken from the abbey in the year 429 as a gift for the pope, who in turn gave them to the Holy Roman Empress, Theophanu, as a wedding gift. She built St Pantaleon's Church in Cologne to house them. Their aura endures to this day. In 2002 a shoulder bone of the saint was given back to St Alban's Abbey and placed in his reconstructed shrine from where all his remains had vanished during the Reformation. The dean of the abbey spoke of the sense of St Alban retuning home, the physical presence of the relic being the focal point of love. Given all the disruptions that the relics of Alban had endured over the centuries, some scepticism about their authenticity could perhaps have been expected. Yet the dean stated that seeking corroboration through carbon testing would not be considered as it would show lack of faith.

In many ways the division of the bodies of royalty was comparable to the distribution of relics of saints, there being great prestige attached to the possession of body parts. The removal of organs for the purposes of the embalming of royalty who may have died far from their chosen burial place was initially driven by necessity due to lack of refrigeration but also created opportunities for multiple burials.

Much of Edward I's belief system now seems remote, primitive even, and religion no longer has the universality that bound communities together in the Roman Catholic England of the thirteenth and fourteenth centuries. Yet the importance that was attached to the ritual of burial in medieval times is a human response that persists. People who are denied an opportunity to bury a loved one speak of their inability to move forward, to grieve fully. We also retain an instinctive feeling that the wholeness of the body should be respected.

*

Edward I displayed overt grief for his wife rather than for his children. To modern sensibilities royal parenting in preceding centuries can appear to be impersonal to the point of indifference. Edward and Eleanor spent a great deal of time apart from their children. When they left England for the Holy Land in 1270, fully expecting to be away for several years, they left three children behind, four-year-old John, two-year-old Henry and one-year-old Eleanor. When they reached Sicily on their return journey they received the news that John had died shortly after his fifth birthday. Soon afterwards they received news of the death of Edward's father, Henry III, to whom Edward was devoted in spite of numerous personal differences. To the surprise of their host, the King of Sicily, it was the death of his father that caused Edward more visible distress. Edward apparently accounted for his response by explaining that while children were replaceable, one's father was unique.

Such an apparently matter of fact attitude towards the death of a child does indeed seem callous to modern sensibilities and even attracted comment at the time. It is perhaps worth bearing in mind that of the fifteen or sixteen children that Eleanor gave birth to, only six outlived her, two more predeceasing Edward. Even by the standards of the thirteenth century Edward and Eleanor were unlucky. We have no way of measuring the strength of the parental bond Edward felt for his children but in his later years he does seem to have shown an affectionate concern for them. Eleanor's attitude to the death of John is not recorded, but it is surely significant that she requested that the heart of her son Alphonso was preserved for burial with her own.

Edward was clearly a man of strong emotions, though they may not have been primarily directed towards his children. Within the aristocracy Edward was unusual in his intense devotion to his wife. It is well known that many royal marriages have been little more than conveniences for the purposes of producing an heir, with romantic love taking place elsewhere, preferably discreetly. Edward was fortunate in that the object of his love was also the woman he was legitimately married to and he was therefore able to make a public statement of his grief.

The romantic nature of their marriage, evinced in part by the building of the crosses, was to take hold in the popular imagination. In the eighteenth and nineteenth centuries Eleanor became the exemplar of everything a queen consort should be, any criticism of her acquisitiveness long forgotten. The Eleanor Crosses were created for the purpose of providing a link between earth and the afterlife. They imply a spiritual dimension, a sense that there is more to life than day to day survival, whatever terms this may be expressed in. Now, as in the time of Edward I, these monuments encourage us to look up, literally and metaphorically, reminding us of the importance to human society of artistic endeavour.

Although the creation of what would now be described as art was vital in the medieval period, it was not expressed in terms of personal fulfilment for an individual artist. The craftsmen of the Middle Ages were people skilled in a trade who were commissioned to harness their talents for the attainment of a preconceived vision. Art had what was considered to be a higher purpose, that of predominantly being a tool for the glorification of God.

The medieval Mass with its multiple appeals to the senses, an experience involving sight, sound, hearing and smell, was intended to touch people in ways that took them beyond themselves. The range of visual stimuli to be absorbed included painting, sculpture, metalwork, stained glass and tapestry, glorious colour revealed by flickering candle light. The imagery was loaded with symbolic meaning that can no longer easily be read. Architecture itself was the realisation of a sacred geometry where numerical systems carried significance. The Church, similarly the garden, represented Heaven on earth. Art was harnessed for the expression of religious devotion with all disciplines of art and craft combining to create an intense, all-embracing experience.

Although the functions of art have changed, the impulses to create, collect and consider art endure. The role for art now, which may include the glorification of God, is much wider than it could have been in the medieval era. For many it has become an end in itself. In the words of the twentieth-century atheist sculptor, Henry Moore, 'artists do not need religion for art is religion itself', suggesting that it is not necessary to believe in an all-powerful creator to feel uplifted by the force of human creativity.

The Eleanor Crosses and the naming of places after them also keep the memory of Queen Eleanor of Castile alive, references to an elusive but real woman who inspired their construction. A great deal about Eleanor's life has been forgotten but it is known with certainty that she died, aged forty-nine, leaving Edward I grief-stricken. Yet his actions did ensure that her name continues to live on while those of so many medieval queens have long been forgotten. Many of the twelve stopping places of the cortège are today full of references to Queen Eleanor, with roads, cafés, newsagents and roundabouts named after her. The towns of Dunstable and Stamford have modern pieces of public sculpture based on Eleanor Crosses. In Dunstable there is a statue of her in the Eleanor's Cross shopping precinct, erected in 1985. Here the queen is seen at eye level, posed in an almond shaped archway, just a small coronet to indicate her royal status. This queen is among the people, touchable, not gazing down on us from on high. The Stamford monument is an elongated cone that repeats the floral pattern of the small fragment that was found. At Stony Stratford there is a smart-looking brass plaque close to the site of the Eleanor Cross. It is fixed to the wall of an unremarkable 1950s private house that looks as if it might collapse under the weight of it.

Although most of the original Eleanor Crosses are lost to us, so many reminders of her can still be discovered. Eleanor of Castile, as Edward intended, lives on, sometimes only in name, sometimes through tangible evidence. As the story of the Eleanor Crosses shows, indicators of the past are all around us and not just in designated places of historical interest. Our towns and cities are multi-layered palimpsests, in some cases harder to read than others, but waiting to be explored and interpreted.

Likewise much information about the life of the Eleanor who inspired the building of the crosses has been lost to us but we can get a sense of this intriguing medieval queen from what is known. Many of the known facts relate directly to King Edward I rather than to Eleanor in her own right but given the strength of their bond inferences can be made.

An imaginative presentation of the life of Eleanor and that unique marriage now follows, piecing together what we know in an attempt to get to the heart of the shared lives of this royal couple over seven centuries ago.

Part III

A MARRIAGE FOR ALL TIME

On leaving northern Spain in 1254 after her marriage to Lord Edward of England at the age of just thirteen, Eleanor of Castile was little more than a pawn in a diplomatic game. Her marriage was simply intended to resolve tensions between England and Castile over the claim to the lordship of Gascony in south-west France. All that was required of Eleanor was to produce an heir to the throne of England. Yet the marriage turned out also to be one of the most enduring royal love matches.

No one could have anticipated that for thirty-six years their personal lives would be so closely and devotedly intertwined. After Eleanor died in 1290 possibly of quartan fever, a form of malaria she had contracted in Gascony, Edward set out to immortalise their marriage in stone. The extraordinary lengths to which he went to commemorate her in the building of the crosses gives tangible evidence of the depth of his love. This is the story of their lives together.

Edward I and Eleanor as depicted in an early-fourteenth-century manuscript (Wikimedia Commons).

11.

ELEANOR'S STORY

In the year 1254 the fifteen-year-old prince Edward Plantagenet, on his first trip overseas, travelled to Castile to meet his future wife, Eleanor of Castile. Lord Edward, as he was then known, was impatient to prove himself and take his place in the diplomatic world of the princes of Christendom. As part of the terms of the marriage he was to be knighted by Eleanor's half-brother, King Alphonso X of Castile and León, and to be assured of his position of Lord of Gascony.

Nineteenth-century engraving of Burgos by Adolphe Rouargue (Wikimedia Commons).

THE ELEANOR CROSSES

Edward arrived in Burgos, a magnificent city in Castile, the wealthiest and most cultured kingdom among the riches of Christian Spain. The royal court where Eleanor had grown up was one of comfort and sophistication. She was used to a life of elegance, with frequent music and dancing, magnificent banquets with abundant fruits, figs, oranges and olives. Even though she was not yet thirteen years old, she was widely read in books of all kinds, psalters, romances and poetry.

The wedding took place with an elaborate ceremony in the convent Abbey of Santa Maria La Real de Las Huelgas. The abbey held personal significance to both her and Edward. It had been founded in 1187 by Alphonso VIII, Eleanor's great-grandfather, and his consort, Eleanor Plantagenet, the sister of Edward's grandfather, King John. In its mausoleum of the royal family of Castile, Edward was fascinated by the exotically carved tombs, so different from those he knew from the cathedrals of England. That of his great-aunt Eleanor was raised on a pedestal of two crouching lions and decorated with heraldic images of the triple-towered castle of Castile.

Although born a thousand miles apart, the young couple found much in common. Both were well taught in Latin and fluent in Court French, the language of the aristocracy. When children, as well as their native tongues both had grown up to learn dialects of French from their mothers in which they were also able to communicate. They shared a love of the same books, tales of chivalry of Alexander the Great, of Charlemagne and in particular, King Arthur of Britain. Most significantly, both were children of kings, with a shared understanding of the privileges and responsibilities their status bestowed on them.

Immediately after the marriage, in spite of the harsh November weather, the couple made the hazardous journey across the Pyrenees to reach Edward's duchy of Gascony. As lord, he was determined to assert his authority and make his mark upon the troublesome Gascon nobility. There they found they had much more in common than royal birth and established a friendship, revelling in freedom from the intrusive supervision of the king and queen of the English court. Their enjoyment was tainted when in May 1255 Eleanor, now just thirteen years old, gave birth to a premature daughter who did not survive.

Their independence was not to last. Edward's mother and father, King Henry and Queen Eleanor, aware of their responsibilities for the young princess' welfare, felt it fitting that the couple should have some time apart until she developed greater physical maturity. Eleanor was instructed to make her way to England while Edward was sent to visit his lands in Ireland.

Eleanor reached England in October 1255, nearly a year after the marriage. Her arrival was marked by a grand ceremonial parade and an elaborate feast. The king and queen went to great pains to make her feel welcome by obtaining her favourite figs and oranges from her homeland, a kindness she was grateful for. The queen, Eleanor of Provence, was particularly solicitous. She herself had arrived in England as a girl, in her case fourteen years old, from a Mediterranean country so different from her new home. She was to meet her future husband for the first time at the wedding ceremony. The queen, like her young namesake, had a fine appreciation of literature and even wrote poetry herself. With a maternal concern for the princess, she went to the expense of making sure the young Eleanor's chambers were comfortable in Castilian style. Ignoring the derision of the English lords, the windows were glazed, carpets provided and the walls hung with thick tapestries.

Edward soon returned to court to be by Eleanor's side, defying his father's orders to go to Ireland, a place that had no appeal for him, being too far removed from the central stage of regal power. Instead he took pride in taking Eleanor on a tour around the country of which they would one day be king and queen. One of the many places they visited was the Abbey of St Albans, accompanying the reigning Queen Eleanor, who wished to make a pilgrimage to the shrine of St Alban to give thanks for her recovery from a recent illness. On that occasion the young Eleanor made an offering of a valuable silk brocade altar cover.

In the summer of 1256 Lord Edward, now seventeen, persuaded his father to hold a tournament in his honour, even though he knew of King Henry's disapproval of such diversions. The king considered tourneying frivolous and indeed dangerous both for the risk of injury and the opportunity it presented for the lords of the realm to meet together and conspire against the monarchy. He was particularly concerned that his headstrong young son would be careless of his own safety. But Edward, by now over six feet tall, strong and highly athletic, was insistent on this opportunity to show off to his young wife his prowess as a horseman and skill with weapons. Henry was forced to concede and the young couple travelled together for the gathering in Nottinghamshire, pleased to be away from the formalities of court. The event was a splendid success, the young men enjoying the exhilaration of the mock battle, careless of the damage to the surrounding countryside. Eleanor and the ladies watched the spectacle unfold from the raised platform that was built for the occasion.

The tournament was followed by a trip to Scotland, for Edward to introduce Eleanor to his younger sister Margaret and her husband the king, Alexander III. This was also an opportunity for Edward to show Eleanor something of the northern parts of England as they made their way. When they arrived they received a warm welcome, enjoying the informality of the company of a king and queen so close to their own ages after the constraints of the English court.

While in Scotland Edward took Eleanor to Whithorn in the south-west of the country, to visit the Priory of St Ninian, Apostle of the South Picts. The priory was one of the greatest pilgrim destinations of Scotland, possessing a shrine with an arm bone of the saint. The visit took place on the feast day of St Ninian, 26 August, an occasion marked by a solemn Mass. Eleanor knew little about this bishop from the early days of Christianity but was intrigued to discover the stories of his miracles, his powers of healing the sick and staying dry while reading his prayer book in the rain.

Those early days of their marriage were not just an occasion for enjoyment. The England that Eleanor arrived in was one of disturbing political unrest with many nobles united in their opposition to the king. The instability rapidly escalated and in 1258 the lords seized power from the king. King Henry suffered the indignity of being stripped of his royal powers by his own magnates. Only thanks to Edward's political skill was royal authority seized back for his father.

The relative peace that followed was short-lived. There was further insurrection just two years later when armed opposition to the monarchy united under the leadership of the Earl of Leicester, Simon de Montfort. The king's army suffered a humiliating defeat at the Battle of Lewes in 1264. The terms of settlement imposed upon the king by the lords were harsh. King Henry was permitted to keep his crown but would have no true authority and was effectively imprisoned. To Edward's fury, he himself was incarcerated in Wallingford Castle, a captive in the kingdom of which he expected to inherit the throne.

Eleanor was held in custody in Windsor Castle with the king and queen. Though she was not subjected to any physical discomfort, she found it deeply shocking that the English lords failed to acknowledge the status due to her as a royal princess of such a cultivated land as Castile. During that time, apart from anxiety over Edward's safety, Eleanor suffered the unhappiness of the death of their only child, the two-year-old Katherine. Soon after, she gave birth to a daughter named Joan. Her prayers that this baby would be strong and healthy were to go unheard for she too died when less than eight months old, never seen by her father.

In May 1265 the irrepressible Lord Edward escaped captivity in Hereford and rallied support against the uprising. De Montfort was killed at the Battle of Evesham, his body ritually mutilated as a traitor. After nearly a year of enforced separation Edward and Eleanor were finally reunited and soon Eleanor was with child again.

Eleanor gave birth to a longed for son in July 1266. The child was named after Edward's grandfather, King John, signatory of the Magna Carta. In choosing the name of that previous unpopular monarch, Edward was making a deliberate reference to the overriding supremacy of the monarchy over the lords of the realm. Nonetheless, the delighted citizens of London declared a holiday to celebrate the occasion, as they had at the time of Edward's birth. The political unrest in England was, for the time being, quelled.

The peace in the realm allowed King Henry to continue work on his grand scheme, the rebuilding of Westminster Abbey. In 1269 a superlative new shrine in the abbey for the relics of the sainted king, Edward the Confessor, was complete. Its consecration was planned for his feast day of 13 October. Lord Edward was proud to take part in this auspicious ceremony, watched by his wife. Eleanor herself was knowledgeable about Edward the Confessor, having studied carefully the accounts of the lives of the notable English saints given to her before her arrival in the country fourteen years previously.

The occasion was marked by a service attended by the highest born of the realm. King Henry, his brother, Richard Earl of Cornwall, and his two sons, the Lord Edward and brother Edmund, carefully removed the remains from the reliquary where they had been put for safekeeping while the building work was progressing. They carefully carried them to their new resting place behind the high altar.

That the shrine of Edward the Confessor should be here was entirely fitting as this was the place that he had chosen to build a magnificent abbey, begun in 1045. He was sanctified in 1163 when King Henry II, anxious that the antecedents of the Plantagenet lineage were given their just acknowledgement, was successful in petitioning Pope Alexander III. Henry III felt a personal connection to the sainted king, to whom he looked as his inspiration and guide, giving him a new prominence among the English saints. He even named his son Edward after him, a name that had long since fallen from favour. On his accession to the throne, Edward I was the first king with an Anglo-Saxon name since before the reign of William the Conqueror over two hundred years earlier.

Even before Edward the Confessor's abbey was built, this ground resonated with spirituality. There had been a church here, on the Island of Thorney, since the dawn of Christianity, itself built on the ruins of a pagan temple. This was a place where people worshipped their gods before the birth of Christ. Matthew Paris, the learned monk of St Albans, retold the story of the life of Edward the Confessor, recounting his vow to St Peter that he would go on pilgrimage to his tomb in Rome if he became King of England. When he did indeed become king, the journey was considered too dangerous and King Edward, later to become the Confessor, asked the pope to release him from his promise if he undertook to rebuild the abbey at Westminster. The pope agreed and building commenced, together with a new palace close by. The abbey was to surpass in size anything previously built in the whole of England.

While it was being built King Edward, surveying the building work, gave a ring to a beggar who stopped him to ask for alms. Two years then passed when in the Holy Land some English pilgrims met an old man who told them he was John, the apostle of Christ. He had in his possession a ring that he asked them to give to King Edward with the message that his life on earth would end within half a year. On their return King Edward recognised the ring as the one he had given the beggar two years previously. Shortly afterwards, King Edward fell ill and was too unwell to attend the ceremony for the consecration of his cathedral. His death soon followed and he was buried in the abbey, the sacred ring on his finger.

During his lifetime the Saxon King Edward was renowned for his piety and generosity to the poor. He was the first King of England gifted with the ability to cure the King's Evil with his touch and could miraculously restore sight to the blind. He also achieved the miracle of ordering the nightingales that were disturbing his study when staying at his hunting lodge to be silent.

The Confessor would not have recognised the abbey as it now was but would undoubtedly have admired the splendours of the new building, begun by the father of Edward I, Henry III. King Henry's vision was to rebuild the abbey as a splendid royal mausoleum, emphasising the links of his royal dynasty with the much venerated Saxon kings. It was intended as a superlative statement of the wealth and importance of the English monarchy. The physical presence of this spectacular building was conceived to show that England was a significant power, with a leading place in the chess game of nations, equal in standing to its French royal cousins.

As she watched the ceremony, Eleanor could not have failed to be impressed by the stupendousness of the abbey, equal to anything in her native Castile.

*

Edward was anxious to prove to Eleanor that he was more than a leader of men in England but was also a celebrated Christian general. His mind was set upon responding to the call to arms issued by Pope Urban IV in 1263 to the princes of Europe to go to the Holy Land, the ultimate goal being the recovery of Jerusalem from Islamic occupation. Even though Lord Edward, as heir to the throne, had been given papal dispensation by Urban's successor, Clement IV, releasing him from the obligation of taking the cross, he was determined to do so. At the Northampton Parliament of 1268 it was agreed that he, his brother Edmund, their cousin, Henry of Almain, and many important lords of the realm should join the venture.

Eleanor was in full support of Edward's ambition to go on crusade. Here was an opportunity for him to make his name and advance the battle of Christianity against the infidel. This noble cause was close to both their hearts. Eleanor's father, King Ferdinand III, was remembered as a hero for reconquering the cities of Seville and Cordoba from the Muslim occupiers of southern Spain for the kingdom of Castile. Edward was fired with tales of the bravery of his great-uncle, King Richard I, the Lionheart, the warrior king who had won back Acre, capital of the Kingdom of Jerusalem, from Islamic control.

Notwithstanding the discomfort of travelling long distances, Eleanor was determined to accompany her husband as many royal wives had done before. On this occasion the heir to the throne of France, Philip, was taking his wife, Isobel, and his sister, Isabella, was accompanying her husband, King Theobald of Navarre. Edward's sister, Beatrice, was going with her husband, John, Duke of Brittany. Eleanor had no wish to be excluded from this party of young royalty. In August 1270 Edward and Eleanor set sail. They left behind them their family, now of three children, in the care of Edward's uncle, Richard of Cornwall.

They finally reached Acre in May 1271, where they found their forces to be impotent against the strength of the Mamluk Muslim occupiers. The crusaders spent long frustrating months in the city, many dying in the intense heat of summer with military action limited to a few minor raids.

Edward and Eleanor found it shocking that in spite of the hostilities Acre was a thriving port where business was good, a crossroads for traders from east and west where Christians openly conducted business with the infidel. Among the many travellers in the city at the same time were Niccolò, Maffeo and Marco Polo at the outset of a journey to the Far East. However widely travelled Edward and Eleanor were themselves they were struck by the tales of the extraordinary bravery of these men, on the brink of a venture into hardly known territory with unimaginable dangers. Niccolò and Maffeo, father and uncle of Marco, had already reached and safely returned from the remote land of China on a previous journey. At the time of Edward and Eleanor's visit they were about to set off for a second journey to the Far East, accompanied by two priests and by Marco, Niccolò's sixteen-year-old son.

Eleanor and Edward would have been intrigued by their stories of exotic people who endured the pains of Purgatory to have pictures in ink made on their skin, of strange fruit, known as apples of paradise, that grew in finger-like bunches. The brothers told how they had met Kublai Khan, ruler of a vast empire at the furthest eastern edge of the world. Edward and Eleanor were puzzled to hear that the emperor revered not only Jesus but also Mohammed, Moses and the Buddhist prophet, Shakyamuni. It was gratifying that Kublai Khan was keen to learn more about Christianity, perhaps a step towards seeing it as the true faith. He had given the Polo brothers a letter for the pope, with a request for a hundred teachers knowledgeable about Christianity to come to educate his people and for an offering of holy oil from Christ's sepulchre in Jerusalem. The brave travellers were now returning to his court with two priests and the requested oil.

Even though there were plenty of distractions, Edward was impatient at the lack of military action. When two of Sultan al-Zahir Baybars' soldiers presented themselves at the English stronghold claiming to be spies from the Muslim court, he was keen to meet them. Once alone with Edward and his interpreter the intruders attempted to stab him with a poisoned blade. It was thanks to Edward's prodigious strength and physical superiority that he was able to kill both his assailants but in the struggle he suffered a deep injury to the shoulder. The wound rapidly became gangrenous, leaving Edward feverish from the poison that entered his body. Fearing the worst, he took the step of preparing his will.

Gustave Doré, *Edward I of England Kills his Would-be Assassin in June 1272* (Wikimedia Commons).

Urgent action was required and Edward's adviser, Otto de Grandson and his brother Edmund, Earl of Lancaster, held him down as the putrid flesh was cut away. Without such an operation he would undoubtedly have died, as had his great-uncle, Richard the Lionheart, from a similar wound. Eleanor was unable to watch his ordeal and was led weeping from the room by the loyal lord of Alnwick, John de Vescy. She herself had just recovered from giving birth to a baby girl, Joan, two months before.

After he had sufficiently recovered and the baby was considered strong enough to travel, Edward was finally persuaded that it was time to leave Acre. The royal party embarked on the eight-week sea voyage to Sicily. Edward and Eleanor were made as comfortable as possible, as befitted a royal couple, but there was no avoiding the lack of privacy and discomfort on the crowded ship. They were taking with them the master builder, John of Acre, who had impressed Edward with the excellent work he had done when commissioned to rebuild the towers of the city walls. While at sea there were long hours of boredom interspersed with the battering of autumn storms that seemed to blow up without warning. Only the baby Joan was able to sleep soundly through all the peaks and troughs of the rough sea as she lay strapped in her cradle.

Edward and Eleanor finally reached Sicily in November 1272, to receive the news that their eldest child, John, had died three months earlier, shortly after his fifth birthday. The New Year followed with news of even greater momentousness. Henry III had died the previous November after a reign of fifty-six years and the Lord Edward was now King of England. Edward mourned deeply the death of his father, a man he continued to hold in respect as a parent in spite of the difficulties that had passed between them.

The new king and queen crossed to the mainland of Italy to begin the long journey back to England. As the royal entourage made its way northwards, through Reggio, Parma and Milan, they were lavishly entertained in a style befitting the new King and Queen of England, crowds flocking to see them on route. They eventually reached the Alps where they crossed the pass of Mont Cenis, to reach the county of Savoy. Even though it was approaching high summer the mountain peaks were capped with snow, the narrow, twisting paths treacherous. Eleanor was pregnant yet again. They eventually arrived at the castle of St Georges d'Espéranche, one of several that belonged to Edward's cousin, Philip, Count of Savoy. Although still incomplete, it was seemingly impregnable, strategically placed with thick concentric walls punctuated with octagonal towers. The imposing construction made a lasting impression on Edward.

From St Georges d'Espéranche they progressed north to Chalon in Burgundy where the count, Peter the Oxherd, invited the English to a tournament. The occasion degenerated into a brawl, with the count failing to observe the rules of chivalry by dragging Edward from his horse by his neck.

*

It was not until August 1274, nearly two years after the death of King Henry and four years after their departure from England, that Edward and Eleanor arrived at Dover. It was a mark of Edward's confidence in his position as the new king of England that he had not felt the need to hurry back for the coronation ceremony.

They were now accompanied by their new-born son, Alphonso, having left the two-year-old Joan in Eleanor's mother's province of Ponthieu in northern France. A large crowd had gathered to meet them, including their older children, Henry and Eleanor, now nearly five and six years old. Slowly the royal entourage progressed towards London, watched by cheering crowds.

Later that month the long awaited coronation in Westminster Abbey took place. It was a glittering spectacle, the first coronation of a monarch in living memory and momentous for being the first occasion that the king and his consort were crowned together. Edward and Eleanor sat in splendour on a wooden platform, raised up so all could see them, high enough that the lords of the realm, mounted on horseback, could ride underneath. Eleanor was to the left of Edward, in acknowledgement of his position of pre-eminence. They began the ceremony dressed in unadorned tunics, the simplicity of Eleanor's dress and her fair hair loose about her shoulders denoting her purity.

Thirteenth-century manuscript: coronation of King Edward I (Chetham's Library, Manchester).

The most sacred part of the ceremony was the act of anointing them with holy oil that had been blessed by the pope, Christ's representative on earth, symbolising the anointing of Biblical King Solomon by Zadok the Priest. Only an archbishop was empowered to carry out this part of the ritual. On this occasion the duty fell to Robert Kilwardby, Archbishop of Canterbury, to pour the oil onto the heads of the king and queen from a golden spoon first used in the coronation of Edward's grandfather, King John. As he did so he spoke the words that had been used since the time of the coronation of the Anglo-Saxon King Edgar by St Dunstan three centuries previously:

Zadok the Priest, and Nathan the Prophet anointed Solomon King
And all the people rejoic'd, and said:
God save the King! Long live the King!

*

Once anointed, the king and queen were endowed with divine recognition of their authority for the offices for which they had been chosen, setting them apart from other mortals. They were truly king and queen by the grace of God.

They were then robed in rich garments. Edward was presented with a magnificent jewelled sword, representing the strength of his temporal rule. In his right hand he took the orb, symbolising the dominion of the Christian faith over the world, the sceptre in his left, for regal authority and justice. The crown of Edward the Confessor was then placed on his head and Eleanor was crowned as queen consort. Once fully attired in the robes of monarchs, Eleanor bowed to the king and the archbishop and all the magnates paid them homage. The ceremony was followed by a sumptuous banquet for thousands of guests, with delicacies such as roasted swan, peacock and crane.

The new king and queen were to make many visits to the abbey for their own personal devotions, often praying at the holy reliquaries that were preserved there. Eleanor herself had occasion to use the girdle of the Virgin Mary to give her strength during childbirth when in confinement at the Palace of Westminster. This sacred item was made and worn by the Virgin herself. At her Assumption she dropped it down from the sky to St Thomas after which it was kept, giving comfort to many royal women during their labours. When Queen Eleanor had need of it, it was taken to her chambers by a special escort of monks. She would return to the abbey after giving birth to offer prayers of thanks for her safe delivery at the churching ceremony when received back into the house of Christ.

Palma il Vechio, *Assumption of the Virgin*, 1514 (Wikimedia Commons). The Virgin is about to drop the girdle down to St Thomas.

Shortly after their coronation Edward and Eleanor went on royal progress throughout the realm. It was important that they should be seen by their subjects and their authority affirmed. One of the many places they returned to was the town of St Albans. At that time the townspeople were in dispute with the abbot, Roger de Norton, who had decreed that they were obligated to use the abbey mill to grind their corn, paying a heavy fee in order to do so. The people took the opportunity to petition Eleanor, now queen and able to intercede on their behalf, her valet translating their grievances into French for her. They begged her to present their side of the case to King Edward. She did so and the king agreed that the matter should be referred to his justices so that both sides could be given a hearing and a fair compromise was reached.

Now king, a duty Edward took on was touching for the King's Evil. On these ceremonial occasions those afflicted with growths on the neck that oozed foul smelling pus would come in their hundreds in search of the healing powers of the king. To Eleanor such a task was deeply repellent. The Kings of Castile were blessed with the power of driving out demons from sufferers but unlike the gift of the Royal Touch, this did not require them to place their hands on the weeping skin of their subjects.

The atmosphere of celebration following the coronation was to be short-lived. Just two months later, in October 1274 the six-year-old Henry died, leaving one-year-old Alphonso as heir apparent. Such a loss was a great personal sadness that also raised concerns regarding Eleanor's future financial security. Should she be widowed she would, as dowager queen, have no entitlement to income from Parliament. If Alphonso were to die too, it was possible that the crown would pass to Edward's brother, Edmund, and his heirs leaving her isolated and vulnerable. It was then that Eleanor began to protect her position through the acquisition of significant property holdings in her own right by taking over debts of landowners who found themselves in financial difficulty.

There was, however, little time for Edward to dwell on personal matters. There were problems in the principality of Wales that required his attention.

*

Edward, as King of England, was the acknowledged overlord of Britain's western peninsula, Wales. The territory was under the rule of princes who were required to pay homage to him in the same way that he himself paid homage to the King of France for the lordship of Gascony. In 1277 a rebellion against the English crown erupted in Wales led by its prince, Llywelyn ap Gruffudd. Unable to defend themselves against English might the Welsh were soon defeated and Edward began a programme of castle building to secure his victory under the supervision of Master James of St George, the builder of the castle of St Georges d'Espéranche that had so impressed Edward when returning from crusade.

Edward knew that the control of Wales could not be achieved by force alone. While the castles established English military strength and provided symbols of English power and domination, Edward needed also to usurp Welsh legend. His battle had not just been with the princes of Wales, but with the legendary King Arthur. While Edward considered the Welsh to be a barbaric people consisting of disorderly bands of wanderers, their princes regarded themselves as the true successors to the heroic King Arthur, whom they believed to be one time king of the whole of the island of Britain.

According to the stories, Arthur could trace his noble ancestry from Brutus, leader of the brave adventurers who discovered Britain when exiled from the ancient city of Troy. In his battles against invaders from the Saxon settlements Arthur had been forced to retreat into the northern and western extremities of the island, to Cornwall, Wales and Scotland. But Arthur was not to be defeated. The people of Wales believed that Arthur was not truly dead, but that his spirit lived on. They lived waiting for the day that he would rise again to reconquer the whole island of Britain and reclaim his rightful kingdom. By these lights it was Edward of England who was the latecomer to the island, the lesser king than their Arthur. These were powerful ideas, not to be defeated by stone and mortar alone.

THE ELEANOR CROSSES

The royal couple marked the occasion of the defeat of the Welsh by visiting Glastonbury Abbey, claimed to be the burial place of King Arthur and his queen, Guinevere, for the translation of their remains to a new, grand tomb. In a solemn ceremony, watched by the monks, the bones were disinterred. Edward respectfully wrapped the bones of Arthur in fine silk while Eleanor did the same for those of Guinevere. They were to be given all the highest honours befitting their royal status. As proof of Edward and Eleanor's acceptance of their authenticity, they stamped the caskets containing the remains with their seals, England asserting its dominance over Wales. The bones were then returned to a simple, imposing tomb chest of Purbeck marble. A king of such renown as Arthur required no ornamentation. King Edward was proving to the people of Wales that it was he who had authority over their King Arthur, that the legendary king was truly dead in body and spirit and would never be returning to rule the British people. There could be no misunderstanding of Edward's message to the Welsh.

While attending the rituals at Glastonbury the king and queen stayed at the manor of Queen Camel that belonged to Edward's mother, held to be the site of Camlann where King Arthur had fought his last battle. Edward and Eleanor took delight in celebrating with an elaborate pageant glorifying the tales of Arthurian chivalry, the king and queen dressed as Arthur and Guinevere.

But peace was to be ephemeral, and in 1282 rebellions in Wales erupted again. To Edward's fury his prized castles were under attack from the Welsh. He retaliated strongly and Llywelyn ap Gruffudd was killed in battle, his brother Daffydd captured and executed as a traitor. Edward was determined that this time his victory would be conclusive and to prove his dominance the severed heads of Llywelyn and Daffydd were prominently displayed at the Tower of London.

The king and queen returned to Wales in the spring of 1284 as undisputed victors. To seal his achievement Edward embarked on a new programme of castle building of unprecedented scale, with strongholds at Conwy, Caernarvon and Harlech. Their imposing presence, louring over the poor dwellings of the Welsh, spoke of the power of England over Wales. As well as being military strongholds, they were provided with luxurious royal apartments and gardens laid out for Eleanor's enjoyment.

All of strategic importance, Caernarvon in particular was emblematic of English domination over the Welsh. The site was selected for Edward's castle for its favourable strategic position on the Menai Straits between Wales and Anglesey. It also made a symbolic connection with the nearby ruins of the Roman legionary fort of Segontium, a Roman stronghold described in legend to have been built by an emperor named Macsen (Magnus Maximus). On the Romans' foray into Wales, he was believed to have married a Welsh princess, Elen, considered to be the mother of the Emperor Constantine. Constantine, held to have been an ancestor of King Arthur, went on to become founder of Constantinople and brought Christianity to Roman Britain.

For the construction of Caernarvon Castle Master James was instructed to use distinctive bands of dark and pale masonry. No mere decorative feature, this was the pattern known to have characterised the walls of the city of Constantinople. The message was evident: an English king was declaring ownership of the Welsh claims to its imperial past.

Not content with building new castles, at Conwy and Caernarvon Edward also laid out whole new towns to be inhabited by English administrators from where they could impose rule on the Welsh. Their comfortable buildings were intended to be the envy of the indigenous people, an assertion of superiority. When bones were discovered during the building of the town of Caernarvon, reputedly those of Emperor Macsen, Edward gave orders that these were to be reburied in his new church, a further statement of his domination.

It was at Caernarvon, in 1284, that the 43-year-old Eleanor gave birth to her last child. The court remained in Caernarvon for three weeks, then still under construction, awaiting the birth, rather than move to the more comfortable Rhuddlan Castle close by. Temporary accommodation for the queen was improved as far as possible, with glass put in the windows of the wooden structure. It was a great relief when a healthy boy was born, named Edward after both his father and the illustrious Edward the Confessor, a quintessentially English prince born in the heart of Wales.

Edward and Eleanor spent that summer on a triumphal tour of Wales, visiting remote places never seen before by an English monarch. In July a spectacular Round Table tournament was held at Nefyn, the place where the prophecies of Merlin were said to have been found. Edward dined with his most trusted nobles around a circular table, re-enacting the scene of Arthur's Camelot. For all the preparation and symbolism, the occasion nearly ended in disaster. There were so many people crowded into the upper floor of the hall for the dancing that it suddenly collapsed. It was astonishing that everyone was able to walk away unharmed. Eleanor assured Edward that this good fortune was a sign from God that his monarchy was blessed.

*

On their return from Wales in 1284 one of the many places they visited was Lincoln for the long awaited consecration of the choir and shrine of St Hugh. The construction of the choir was begun in 1220 shortly after the canonisation of the former bishop and took sixty-five years to complete. Pope Martin IV had been sufficiently concerned about the delay in providing this revered saint with a suitable resting place that he decreed that there should be a forty-day remission from Purgatory for all those contributing to the fabric fund for the building of the choir or who attended the occasion of the translation of his relics. At long last enough money was raised to complete the choir in a way that would be worthy of the saint.

At the consecration ceremony the Archbishop of Canterbury, John Pecham, and no fewer than eight other distinguished bishops were present. As prayers were chanted for St Hugh his body was placed in its resting place, a shrine decorated with silver, gold and precious gem stones. His head, which had become severed from the body, was encased in a coffer of silver and gold and placed beside the altar of John the Baptist.

That same year the king and queen were able to spend a whole week at Leeds Castle in Kent, one of their favourite residences. Eleanor acquired Leeds Castle in 1278 from William Leyburn, a knight in the king's household, as payment in settlement of his debts. Together she and Edward devised many improvements, enlarging the suites of private rooms, even providing a bathroom in Castilian fashion, creating gardens and an attractive lake. It was on one such stay that Edward made a bet with his laundress, Matilda, that she would not be able to ride one of his war-horses. When she succeeded he happily paid what he owed.

*

Edward and Eleanor had returned from Wales in possession of many trophies of the Princes of Wales. Among them was Arthur's Crown, a coronet worn by generations of Welsh princes that Edward instructed the royal goldsmith to embellish. In 1285 their eldest son, the ten-year-old Prince Alphonso, undertook his first official role and presented it at the shrine of Edward the Confessor in Westminster Abbey.

The Eleanor Crosses

Alphonso's sudden death just a few months later was a shocking blow to the king and queen, leaving a vulnerable baby a few months old as next in line to the throne. The loss of their son and heir, apparently a thriving boy and not a helpless infant, was a devastating misfortune. That the date of Alphonso's death was the anniversary of Edward and Eleanor's coronation was doubly unsettling.

With Eleanor now in her mid-forties, after sixteen pregnancies her child bearing years at last came to an end. With just one surviving son, having lost three, the succession was a matter of pressing concern. Edward called a meeting at which Eleanor, his mother, senior churchmen and lords of the realm were present. Although there was no precedent for a Queen of England being crowned in her own right it was agreed that in the event of the death of his son, Edward of Caernarvon, the succession should pass to their eldest surviving daughter, at that time the Princess Eleanor. It was hoped that having plans in place would avoid the country descending into chaos in the unfortunate eventuality that there was no male successor to King Edward.

Wishing to restore confidence in the symbolism of the monarchy, Edward made preparations for an elaborate ceremony in the following year of 1285, the presentation at Westminster Abbey of the Cross of Neith. This the greatest of the Welsh treasures was a fragment of the True Cross, the very cross on which Christ was crucified. It was found in the early years of Christianity by St Helena, known to the Welsh as Elen, mother of Emperor Constantine, when on pilgrimage to the Holy Land. While there she identified the site of Golgotha and ordered the ground to be excavated. Three indistinguishable crosses were dug up. She was able to single out the actual cross on which Christ was crucified by placing a corpse in contact with each in turn. The dead man was miraculously brought back to life when touching the one true cross. Alongside it, she found three nails.

Edward and Eleanor were immensely proud of their trophy which thereafter they paraded with them for all to see on their progress throughout the kingdom. Each Good Friday King Edward used it in the ritual of the veneration of the cross, prostrating himself in front of it and crawling up towards it in an act of adoration.

Also in 1285, in spite of Queen Eleanor's protestations, their six-year-old daughter Mary and her cousin Eleanor took the veil at Amesbury Priory in Wiltshire. It was here that the dowager queen, Eleanor of Provence, was planning to retire and was insistent on having two of her granddaughters there for company. Edward on this occasion supported his mother's wishes over those of his wife. Eleanor's anger was only assuaged with the assurance that Mary should be well endowed with land in order to provide her with regular supplies of fuel and wine. Becoming a Bride of Christ notwithstanding, the royal princess would not endure any physical discomfort.

With confidence in the monarchy restored following the death of Alphonso, the king and queen returned to Gascony. It was a clear indication of the strength of King Edward's authority that he could entrust the rule of the country to his lords while he was away. The court celebrated Christmas of 1287 in Bordeaux, where Edward gave Eleanor a beautiful chess set. In the early months of the following year Edward named one of the many new Gascon settlements that he had founded, the now vanished Burgus Reginae, known in England as Queensborough, in her honour.

Easter 1287 was memorable for an occurrence that exemplified King Edward's good fortune. On Easter Sunday the company was assembled in a room at the very top of a tower, which was suddenly struck by lightning. The floor collapsed, falling eighty feet to the ground. Three knights were killed while the king merely suffered a broken collar bone. That this dramatic event took place on such an auspicious day was surely a sign that Edward's life was spared for a particular purpose. This was not the first time he had been saved in such a way. On one occasion in his youth he had been playing chess and stood up to stretch his legs, only for a piece of masonry to fall on the exact spot where he had been sitting.

Much of their stay in Gascony was taken up by a dispute between the Kings of France and Aragon over claims to the throne of Sicily, with King Edward acting as mediator. During 1288 the king and queen travelled to the southern border of Gascony with northern Spain to meet a delegation from Aragon. A settlement was reached, part of which required Edward to hand over seventy-six hostages, including Otto de Grandson and several other high standing members of the English court. By February of the following year Edward had raised money and replacement hostages and he and a few close advisers set off across the Pyrenees for Aragon to deliver them. The mountains were still virtually impassable at that time of year and Eleanor had to accept that this was one occasion when she could not travel with her husband. Instead she spent the next month praying for Edward's safe return. He at last returned unharmed, to the delight of the English court and great relief of Eleanor.

In June 1289 Edward and Eleanor, after an absence of over three years, set off from Gascony to return to England, where his strong leadership was required once more. Two months later, the royal couple arrived at Dover, met by their five daughters and five-year-old Prince Edward. Little did they know that when abroad Eleanor had contracted a disease which would kill her in a little more than a year's time.

On their return Edward and Eleanor made their devotions at the shrines of East Anglia which they often visited. They stopped at the holy places of Waltham Abbey, Bury St Edmunds and Ely, following the pilgrimage route to Walsingham. Edward held Walsingham in particular affection as it was the place where he had given thanks after one of several miraculous escapes from death in his youth. Eleanor also felt a special connection to Walsingham as among its revered treasures was a vial containing the milk of the Virgin Mary, her soul touched by the bond of motherhood.

The task now incumbent upon them, a matter concerning both state and family, was the planning of the marriages of two of their five surviving daughters. First, in the spring of 1290, was the long awaited wedding of eighteen-year-old Princess Joan of Acre to the forty-six-year-old Gilbert de Clare, Earl of Hertford and Gloucester. The marriage took place in a private ceremony, a union intended to resolve differences between the king and the magnates. It was celebrated with a tournament at Winchester Castle for which Edward commissioned a vast round table of oak, eighteen feet in diameter, where he and his lords feasted in the spirit of Camelot, dressed in the robes of King Arthur and his knights.

The following summer the marriage of Princess Margaret to John, heir to the Dukedom of Brabant, Lothier and Limbourg, took place. This was a glittering state ceremony, a display to reaffirm the strength of Edward's rule. Both aged fifteen, Princess Margaret and John had been betrothed since they were three years old. Eleanor had only reluctantly agreed to the marriage of her daughter at such a young age but accepted the timing as necessary.

Nearly a thousand Londoners attended the ceremony alongside the lords and ladies of the realm and royalty from overseas. The festivities continued with a splendid feast at which the guests were entertained with extravagant displays of harpists, violinists, minstrels, acrobats and jesters. Among their number was the famous acrobatic dancer, Matilda Makejoy, who had entertained the court on many important occasions.

That autumn the royal entourage travelled to Clipstone in Nottinghamshire to attend Parliament. While there the queen was able to enjoy the comfortable new chambers and private chapel that the king had built for their personal use. As ever he had been busy with government affairs, the lords all trying to attract his personal attention. Even so, there had been opportunity for diversions, time to spend together enjoying the hunt in Sherwood Forest.

With the business of Parliament concluded, the king and queen, satisfied with a job well done and optimistic for the future, set off for Scotland where Edward had been invited to give advice on the matter of the succession.

The Eleanor Crosses

*

That journey was never completed.

King Edward and Queen Eleanor got no further than the village of Harby in Northamptonshire. Eleanor of Castile died on 27 November 1290, aged forty-nine, in terror of the afterlife that awaited her.

She left Edward grief-stricken and charged with the responsibility of safeguarding the onward passage of her soul. It is thanks to his commemorative legacy that Eleanor is still remembered.

GAZETTEER OF THE CROSSES

Lincoln, Lincolnshire
Built by Richard of Stow
Destroyed during dissolution of the monasteries
Part of statue survives, now in Lincoln Castle

Grantham, Lincolnshire
Builder not known
Destroyed during English Civil War
No traces remain

Stamford, Lincolnshire
Builder not known
Destroyed during English Civil War
Possible fragment survives, now in Stamford Museum

Geddington, Northamptonshire
Builder not known
Stands in centre of village of Geddington
Damaged, some restoration 1920s

Hardingstone, Northamptonshire
Built by John of Battle, carving by William of Ireland
Stands on outskirts of Northampton, near Queen Eleanor Roundabout
Restored during eighteenth and nineteenth centuries

Stony Stratford, Milton Keynes
Built by John of Battle
Destroyed during English Civil War
Commemorative plaque on Stony Stratford High Street

THE ELEANOR CROSSES

Woburn, Bedfordshire	Built by John of Battle, carving by Ralph de Chichester Destroyed No traces remain Woburn Abbey built over original site
Dunstable, Bedfordshire	Built by John of Battle Destroyed Modern statue of Eleanor in Quadrant Shopping Centre, Broadwalk, Dunstable
St Albans, Hertfordshire	Builder not known Partially destroyed during English Civil War, rest demolished in eighteenth century Commemorative plaque on High Street
Waltham, Hertfordshire	Built by Roger of Crundale, carving by Alexander of Abingdon Stands in Waltham Cross town centre Much damaged and heavily restored, further damage during World War II Statue preserved in V&A collection
Cheapside, London	Built by Michael of Canterbury Destroyed during English Civil War Fragment survives in Museum of London
Charing, London	Built by Richard of Crundale, carving by Alexander of Abingdon Destroyed during English Civil War

BIBLIOGRAPHY

Numerous books have informed different aspects of *The Eleanor Crosses*. These are some of the key sources:

GENERAL HISTORICAL INFORMATION:
Oxford Dictionary of National Biography: oxforddnb.com
British History Online: british-history.ac.uk
David Hugh Farmer, *The Oxford Dictionary of Saints*, Oxford University Press, 1987.

EDWARD I AND ELEANOR OF CASTILE:
Sara Cockerill, *Eleanor of Castile: The Shadow Queen*, Amberley, 2014.
Marc Morris, *A Great and Terrible King: Edward I and the Forging of Britain*, Hutchinson, 2008.
John Carmi Parsons, *Eleanor of Castile: Queen and Society in Thirteenth-Century England*, Macmillan, 1995.
Michael Prestwich, *Edward I*, Methuen, 1988.

MEDIEVAL ATTITUDES TO DEATH:
Paul Binski, *Medieval Death: Ritual and Representation*, British Museum Press, 1996.
T.S.R. Boase, *Death in the Middle Ages: Mortality, Judgement and Remembrance*, Thames and Hudson, 1972.
Jacques Le Goff, *The Birth of Purgatory*, Scolar Press, 1984.

MEDIEVAL ART AND SOCIETY:
Jonathan Alexander and Paul Binski (eds), *Age of Chivalry: Art in Plantagenet England, 1200-1400*, Royal Academy of Arts, 1987.
David Gentleman, *A Cross for Queen Eleanor*, London Regional Transport, 1979.

Sophia Menache, *The Vox Dei: Communication in the Middle Ages*, Oxford University Press, 1990.

David Parsons (ed.), *Eleanor of Castile, 1290-1990: Essays to Commemorate the 700th Anniversary of her Death*, Paul Watkins, 1991.

Marjorie and C.H.B. Quennell, *A History of Everyday Things in England, 1066-1499*, Batsford, 1922.

REFORMATION:

Eamon Duffy, *The Stripping of the Altars: Traditional Religion in England, 1400-1580*, Yale University Press, 1992.

WESTMINSTER:

Peter Rex, *King and Saint: The Life of Edward the Confessor*, The History Press, 2008.

A.L.N. Russell, *Westminster Abbey*, Chatto & Windus, 1943.

Robert Shepherd, *Westminster: A Biography*, Bloomsbury 2012.

INDEX

The twelve Eleanor crosses are marked in bold type, to aid longitudinal studies of each.

THE ELEANOR CROSSES